NOTTINGHAMSHIRE PLACE NAMES

ANTHONY POULTON-SMITH

First published 2009

The History Press
The Mill, Brimscombe Port
Stroud, Gloucestershire, GL5 2QG
www.thehistorypress.co.uk

British Library Cataloguing in Publication Data.
A catalogue record for this book is available from the British Library.

ISBN 978 0 7524 4888 6

Typesetting and origination by The History Press
Printed in Great Britain

Contents

Introduction

Nottinghamshire's place names have been influenced by its history. Standing close to the border between Saxon- and Scandinavian-controlled England, it has influences from both languages. Indeed, there are numerous examples of both tongues combining to form a single place name.

Prior to this, the Roman and Celtic tongues prevailed. While the Roman influence can be seen dotted around the county, Latin did not offer much towards the place names. However, the Celtic tongues are very common in the names of hills and streams, much the same as elsewhere in England. Little is known of these Celtic tongues for there is no written record, yet there is the chance to make comparisons with Welsh, Cornish and Breton, all of which are still spoken to some degree, and which can often provide the answer to an ancient hill or stream name. These names from the landscape of hills and streams are normally very simplistic and can be defined as 'hill', 'ridge', 'summit' and 'water', 'flowing', river'. Before questioning these definitions, remember how the local river or hill is still referred to as such today, rarely do locals mention such by name. In days when travel was the exception, such references would have never seemed unusual.

To find the meaning of a place name depends, to some degree on, what it is the name of. Towns, villages, roads, streets, and even houses have to be traced in as many documents as possible; the older the forms the better. Often the earliest records are lost, in which case a little experience is necessary to predict the earlier forms from those known. Geographical features require knowledge of Celtic languages and a simple glance at the area, especially if it can be visualised as it would have appeared when the name first appeared. Public houses are a quite different subject altogether and require looking at from unusual angles.

When speaking of old records, invariably Domesday comes to mind. However, it is a notoriously inaccurate source for place name forms and with good reason. The details of land, produce, etc. is common to most entries, making the number of different words remarkably small. Indeed it is only the proper names which are different. During a time when few could read and write, information was being given by those speaking a Germanic tongue to the officers conducting the survey who spoke Norman French, a language from the Latin group, and as they would have been unlikely to be co-operative with each other, the accuracy is at best questionable.

Streets and roads take their names from a number of sources. The oldest names may seem to be named after the field or place they run to and/or from. However, these shorter lanes more often mirror the region they run alongside which seems somewhat confusing to us in the modern era. In later years, the development of our towns and cities meant houses were being built on a scale never previously seen. Those who funded the development would give the names of their friends and family to these streets. In recent times the new developments on the outskirts of a town or village are taken from the names of the fields on earlier maps, while slum clearances and factory demolitions in urban areas are often named after the industries and characters who previously lived there.

When it comes to pubs, the names can come from a great many different areas. Initially the sign, and therefore the name, was simply a stake or trunk of a tree on the road outside a farm where ale was brewed. It was often unwise to drink the water and thus ale was the staple tipple offered to travellers. It was advertised by tying a sheaf of barley to the post or 'ale stake' at the side of the road which, as a major ingredient in brewing, advertised it as a refreshment station and is the forerunner of the modern pub sign and, by extension, the name.

In later years, signs became more intricate and inns sought increasingly subtle ways to attract customers by reflecting the area, ownership, political persuasion, trades, famous individuals and events; indeed, anything which would make their premises unique and the most desirable drinking house. The tree itself was an obvious subject as well as patriotic names, the monarchy and the landscape. Coats of arms, such as those of trades common to the area or the landlord in his earlier career, or often of the family who owned the land were popular pub name originations. More often, just a part of those arms were used, which is why there are so many coloured animals in pub names. Indeed, the Red Lion is the most common in the land, with over six hundred examples.

In producing this book I would like to thank all those who made some contribution, however small. The librarians of the county of Nottinghamshire, the individuals from societies and historical groups whose knowledge provided the smallest detail, the archivists whose diligent work prevented me from spending hours searching through cuttings and articles, the landlords who related some delightful anecdotes behind the names of their establishments, and the people who pointed me in the right direction when I was lost.

A

Alverton

There are two references to this place in 1086, as *Aluritone* and *Aluretun*. A century later and the name appears exactly as it does today and yet, as if to prove that phonetic spelling and understanding were the norm, a record from 1716 informs us this place was known by the completely different name of *Overton*! In fact the origin here is nothing like the eighteenth-century record, this place began life as 'Aelfhere's farmstead'.

Annesley

This name is recorded as *Aneslei* in 1086, *Anisleia* in 1190, *Annesleia* in 1194, and *Anelegh* in 1220. There is no doubt this comes from the Old English 'An's woodland clearing', featuring a very common suffix *leah*.

The first element is given as a personal name, yet there is a small possibility it could be *an* meaning 'one'. While there is no doubt it fits the clues, it fails to satisfy the basic requirement of any name. The only reason to give anything a name is so it is unique, otherwise everywhere would simply be called 'Home' and everyone 'Me'. With the many *leahs* in the land, a name telling us it was 'one clearing' would hardly be unique.

To the west of here is the **Cuttail Brook**, a name listed in 1235 as *Cotelbroke* and yet which remains undefined. It is without doubt of Saxon origin and will be related to the German *Kutzelbach* and *Kuttelbach*, yet none of these have ever been explained.

Other local names include **Garfit House**, from Old English *gor* and Old Scandinavian *thwaite* giving us '(the place at) the muddy clearing'. A similar meaning is found from the Old English *meos leah* giving us the 'marshy clearing' and which has evolved to become **Mosley Farm**.

The local pub here is the **Badger Box**, a unique name with a very unusual etymology. During the period around the end of the Second World War the landlord kept a badger in a specially constructed box. Minnie, as the pet was called, proved a great attraction until one day the box was found empty. The badger was never seen again and presumed to have returned to the wild. In order to perpetuate the name, a stuffed badger was acquired and displayed in a glass case inside the establishment.

Arnold

There is no question that this is from the Saxon *earn* + *halh*, although Domesday's spelling shows this as *Ernehale*. As with all such places anywhere in the country, the name can be defined as 'the nook of land where eagles are seen'.

Minor place names within this area include **Cockcliffhill Farm** which, if defined today without the benefit of our knowledge of our ancestral languages, would probably not be understood as coming from '(place at) the rounded hill'. **Dorket Head** means 'valley road' from Old Scandinavian *dalr* and *gata*, the additional 'head' telling us it stood at the head of the valley. In 1689, William Surgy was living here, his name being taken for the lane where he lived and four centuries later still appears as **Surgeys Lane**.

Ramsdale Farm may seem obvious and may indeed be 'the valley where rams or wethers are kept.' Clearly wethers (castrated male sheep) are destined for the dinner table, and while such is not unheard of, in reality this was not often seen before the Middle Ages. Therefore the true origin is probably either 'the valley of the ravens', or maybe the term for this bird was used as a personal name and thus should be given as 'Rafn's valley'.

Bonington Road recalls Richard Parks Bonington. The nineteenth-century painter was a member of the English school of watercolourists and was born here in October 1802. Similarly, the names of **Hallams Lane**, **Hickling Lane** and **Thackeray Lane** were named after families who were resident in each at various times through history. **Woollitas** was the name given to a large field with a pond, constructed with the specific purpose of washing sheep. Finally there is **Stockings Farm**, not, as it would seem, a personal name but a reference to a former farmer who also had a shop of stocking frames. This was the basic wooden framework used in the woollen textiles industry which was invented by William Lee of Calverton, less than 3 miles from here.

Public houses around Arnold of note include the **Burntstump Inn**, named after the hill which undoubtedly in turn took its name from a local feature. Indeed it is possible the stump was created as a marker for some unknown reason. **The Flying Horse** is ultimately a reference to Pegasus, the winged horse of Greek mythology. In the case of pub names it is always heraldic, most often found in association with the Knights Templar although there does not seem to be any direct link in this case. Meanwhile, the **Ram Inn** is associated with the coat of arms of the Worshipful Company of Clothworkers and in particular the wool trade. One of the most popular pub names in the land honours one of its greatest heroes. Built in 1923 the **Lord Nelson** shows how, a century after his death, his popularity remained as high as ever. The **Friar Tuck Inn** is taken from the stories told of Robin Hood, this figure being popular because of his happy disposition. No surprise to find other members of Sherwood Forest's legendary band of outlaws are featured in the **Robin Hood and Little John**.

Ashfield

The only record of note is that of *Esfeld* in 1216. This is undoubtedly from Saxon *aesc* + *feld* meaning 'open land where ash trees grow'.

Askham

Records of this name begin with Domesday's *Asca, Ascham Archiepiscopi* in 1167, and *Askham* in 1289. The name comes from the Saxon *aescham* meaning 'ash tree farm' and has obviously been influenced by the Scandinavian tongue. The listing from the twelfth century shows it was an outlying estate or berewick of Laneham, which was held by the Archbishops of York until the nineteenth century.

Locally we find **Stocking Lane**, from the Middle English *stocking* meaning 'stump clearing' and rough ground making farming or building difficult. There is also **Nancy Fox Field** and **Nancy Fox Lane**. While no record of a Nancy remains we do find a mention of Joseph and Richard Fox who were tenants here in 1840. It is a reasonable assumption that Nancy was a relative, probably an ancestor.

One pub here takes its name from a time when patriotism and allegiance were shown not by a written sign as few could actually read, but by hanging out a pub sign bearing a **Rose and Crown**.

Aslockton

This name is from the Old English tongue spoken by the Saxons, the suffix being the common *tun*. Domesday lists the place as *Aslachestone* and the spelling of *Aselakeston* in found almost a century later. However, the personal name is a Scandinavian one. This is not unusual, hybrid names are in fact quite common. Here the origins are in 'the farmstead of Aslakr'.

Within this area are two names which tell us something about the history of this place. Without further evidence there is only one possible explanation for the name of **Cocker Bridge**. This is the bridge which allows us to cross the Smite and should be named as such. Therefore the river here must have once been known as the Coker, a certainly fitting name for it means 'crooked, winding'.

We also find **Speller Hill** at the highest point and at a crossroads. Undoubtedly this was the assembly point for the meeting of representatives from this area and thus the meaning is 'hill of speech'.

The pub here is **The Cranmer Arms**, named after Thomas Cranmer who was born in this village in 1489. He served as Archbishop of Canterbury under Henry VIII and Edward VI, but was doomed when Mary Tudor ascended the throne. A staunch Catholic, 'Bloody' Mary, as she became known, had him burned at the stake after being found guilty of heresy.

Attenborough

Listed as *Aedingburc* in 1205, *Adingburg* in 1229, and as *Adinburcha* in 1339. These forms make it difficult to define the personal name with any certainty. Undoubtedly the second and third elements are from Saxon *inga* + *burh*, which gives us 'the stronghold of the people or followers of Adda or Aeddi'.

Averham

Found as *Aigrum* in 1086, *Aegrum* in 1200, *Egrum* in 1227, and *Averum* in 1316, the modern form is a corruption of Old English *egor* or its plural *egrum*. The name means '(place by) the floods', a reference to the Trent which, as discussed under its own entry, means 'wanderer', i.e. 'liable to flood'.

Averham has its own watercourse which joins the Trent nearby. It goes by the name of **Pingley Dyke**. Listed in 1589 as *le Pingle dike*, the name comes from the Middle English *pightel* meaning 'the small enclosure with a ditch'.

Minor place names include **Mickleborough Hill**, which comes from Old English *micel beorg* meaning 'the place at the big hill'. **Flash Farm** tells us there were a number of springs here; indeed these are still seen today. Finally **Frog Abbey**, which does not refer to the amphibian but to the preferred habitat of that creature – i.e. 'marshy land'.

Awsworth

The value of finding records of a name prior to the Norman Conquest is illustrated by this place. Listed in Domesday as *Eldesvorde*, the personal name here would have been uncertain were it not for the record from 1002 as *Ealdeswyrthe*. Admittedly the spelling of the Saxon suffix of *worth* was subjected to an individual's personal preference, yet there can be no doubt this is 'the enclosure of a man called Eald'.

The local here is **The Hog's Head** which, irrespective of what is depicted on the sign, always refers to the large cask used specifically for beers and wines. Oddly there is no standard measurement for this container, although it is rarely sold in such today.

B

Babworth

Domesday gives this place name as *Baburde*, which by the twelfth century had become *Babbeuurde*, and in 1294 as *Babbewrth*. This is clearly from Saxon *worth*, giving 'the enclosure of a man called Babba', a popular personal name of the time.

Within the parish we find names such as **Ranby**, an Old Scandinavian name speaking of 'the *by* or village of a man named Hrani'. There are remnants of the names of former residents such as **Kippax Lodge** where the family of George Kippax lived in about 1840. Here, too, is **Forest House**, not exactly a family name but a reminder that Babworth stands on the borders of Sherwood Forest. However, the forest did give its name to a resident for in 1332 one Edward de la Forest is recorded as having his home here. As with many parishes there is the humorous 'remoteness' name, here in the extreme north-east is found **Botany Bay**.

Balderton

Early listings give this name as *Baldretone* in 1086 and *Baldertun* in 1160, clearly from the Saxon *tun* and meaning 'the farmstead of Baldhere'.

While the so-called 'remoteness' names are found in many parishes, they usually refer to the most distantly held lands of the former British Empire. The name of **Jericho Lodge** is by no means a typical example of such a name, yet there seems to be no other possible explanation.

Barnby-in-the-Willows

Records of this name are limited to Domesday's *Barnebi*. This, and other places similarly named, have never been defined with any certainty. The most obvious origin is a Scandinavian personal name such as Barni or Bjarni, although there is also the Old Scandinavian word *barn* meaning 'children'. If the true origin is *barn* + *by*, then this is 'the farmstead of the children (i.e. heirs)'. Without further examples the definition will remain uncertain. The addition literally means 'among the willow trees' and is to differentiate from other places similarly named.

The **Witham River** here, which is only in the county for a short part of its course, is recorded as *Wioma* in 1000, *Widme* in 1150 and *Withma* in 1150. However, the name is certainly much older than this, indeed it is referred to by the Greek writer Ptolemy as *Widumanios*. Taking into consideration the different languages involved, this ancient Greek record may show this is Welsh *gwydd* 'woodland' with Latin *manare* 'to flow'. Today there is very little woodland left, yet two thousand years ago the name would have been most appropriate.

Minor names around this place have varied origins. **Shire Dyke**, for example, is clearly a reference to its position on the county boundary, but it is unusual to find it as a place name. Former residents here include Edward Kellet who was here in 1660 and gave his name to **Kelwick Farm**, while **Browne's Wood** was on or near the domain of Christopher Browne who was farming here in 1850.

The name of **Flawford Farm** seems to be taken from a river crossing of that name which was once found here. Undoubtedly the first element is Old English *flor* meaning 'pavement' and the second Old Scandinavian *flaga* 'slab of stone'. In combination it is easy to see how the former was made from the latter. However, despite the modern name, there never has been a 'ford' here and thus it is a corruption. Indeed the meaning from the name indicates that this was a house which had a stone floor.

Barnby Moor

As with the previous entry, the meaning of the basic name is difficult because of the lack of early forms. Indeed the record of this place is exactly the same as Barnby in the Willows, being listed *Barnebi*, and is also found in Domesday. Thus the best guess is 'the farmstead of the children or heirs', while the addition is an obvious reference to its location on moorland.

Locally we find the district of **Bilby**, a name of Old Scandinavian origins in 'Billi's *by* or settlement'.

Barnstone

Two early forms of this name show that the suffix is Old English *tun* 'farmstead' and not *stan* meaning 'stone'; the modern spelling is merely a corruption. Domesday's *Bernestune* and as *Berneston* in 1169 help us to define this place as 'Beorn's farmstead'.

Barton in Fabis

The basic name is a very common one, hence most are found with an addition. While there are two possible origins, either Old English *baer* + *tun* 'the barley farm' or *bere* + *tun* 'outlying grange where corn is stored', the idea is fundamentally the same – i.e. this region was agricultural, probably with good quality soil, used exclusively for growing and storing grains.

For the addition we only need to examine the early records. That of *Bartone* in Domesday is of little help, yet by 1388 we find *Barton in le Benes*. This latter listing is exactly the same as the modern form, *in Fabis*, itself simply the Latin for 'where beans are grown'.

One local name is rather unusual. On the face of it **Garbythorpe** is nothing special, indeed it is not until we define the name that we see how different it is. The *thorpe* refers to an 'outlying farmstead' and is a common Old English term. The first element is a personal name, one Gerbod de Eschaud, the Norman French landlord. This individual is the unusual factor for, unlike virtually every other personal name found in place names throughout the land, this individual is documented. Little is known of his life and family, except for when he came to this part of Nottinghamshire and his family's origins.

Road sign at Barton in Fabis.

Basford

Actually two places, **Old Basford** and **New Basford**; the two are very close together and have a history which is inextricably linked. Early records show the name as *Baseford* in 1086, *Basceford* in 1246, *Baseforth* in 1246, *Besseford* in 1302, and *Basfard* in 1539 and is undoubtedly from 'Basa's ford', a crossing of the River Leen.

Carrington is named after an individual. Local banker Robert Smith was created Lord Carrington in 1796. He owned 3 hectares of land between the modern A60 and A611 and it is this land which brought the name to Basford. **Cinderhill** may be a little obvious, yet this name tells us more than simply 'the fire residue on the hill'. Only a short search through the history of the region revealed that lime kilns stood on a ridge of land near the Colliers Arms. Finally, the name of **Mapperley** is a place name which was taken as a personal name by Thomas Mapperley. He was lord of the manor here during the reign of Richard II and, from what was written of him, he was a well-respected individual.

The Newcastle Arms refers to the Duke of Newcastle, who not only owned extensive lands in the county but served as Lord Lieutenant. Always eager to show a patriotic leaning in order to attract similarly minded customers, landlords found the **Standard of England** a readily available symbol and something a little different from the norm. Most animals in pub signs are heraldic, which is why there are so many oddly coloured animals in pub names. Indeed it is so normal to see such that when we find **The Lion** it stands out, even though it is also heraldic and representative of England.

'Horse' names have always been popular for pubs, ever since the days of the coaching houses. Clearly it would be confusing to have dozens of pubs within a catchment having the same name, so landlords were always looking for the little something extra. Hence we have pubs in the town called **The Horse and Groom** and the **Horse and Jockey. The Elm Tree** doubtless stood near the site of such a marker, and may well have been a part of the original sign itself.

Bassingfield

Early records for this name are as *Basingfelt* in 1086, *Basingefeld* in 1265, and *Bassingfeld* in 1285. This Old English place name is derived from a personal name, together with *inga* + *feld*. Here is 'clearing of the family or followers of Bassa'.

Bathley

This name was recorded as *Badeleie, Badelee,* and *Batheleg* in the eleventh, twelfth and thirteenth centuries respectively. There can be little doubt this is from the Old English *baeth* + *leah* and giving 'the woodland clearing where springs were used for bathing'.

Once again, defining a place name gives an instant image of life in Saxon times, although it is likely your mind pictured a summer scene and not some poor individual bathing in a biting northerly wind in icy waters on a gloomy January morning!

The village local is **The Crown Inn**, one of many throughout the land which shows a sense of patriotism and which most often refers to it being built on land belonging to the monarch.

Beckingham

A name found in Domesday as *Bechingeha*, in 1187 as *Bekingeham*, in 1204 as *Bechingham*, and in 1252 as *Begingham*. Undoubtedly this tells us of 'the homestead of the family or followers of Becca'.

Locally we find **Tong's Wood**, telling us here were 'tongues of land' and referring to land around the wood, not within. There is also the name of **Tetheringrass Lane**, which really did lead to where animals were tethered to partake of the pasture.

Beeston

A fairly common name, mostly derived from the Old English *beos* + *tun*, 'the farmstead where bent grass is seen'. This definition should be understood that the 'bent grass' is a natural phenomenon, not trampled down but having grown tall and collapsed through the wind and rain.

The Durham Ox is a pub name recalling the animal bred by Charles Collings of Darlington. The ox was sold for the sum of £250 and, by the time it was six years old, weighed almost 2 tons. The new owner adapted a vehicle to transport the animal around and, despite the outlay, made a substantial profit. The name is found in places visited by the magnificent beast.

The Hop Pole would have been an easily recognised sign in the early days; passers-by would have understood that ale was brewed where it was shown. Other trades reflected in names here include **The Nurseryman** and **The Beekeeper**. Sports and games have always been closely associated with pubs, if not where they took place but as a meeting point. Locally we find examples of each in **The Cricketers** and **The Double Top**. **The Commercial** may not seem it, but it was originally intended as an invitation to commercial travellers as a place to meet others.

Besthorpe

There are at least two places known as Besthorpe in England, the other being in Norfolk. Both have limited early records and have proven difficult to define. The

Nottingham version is only found as *Bestorp*, albeit three times from three different centuries. That the origins have been influenced by the Scandinavians is certain, the suffix being *thorp* 'the outlying farmstead'. However, the first element could be either the personal name Bosi, a Scandinavian name, or could be from Saxon *beos* 'bent grass'. Such hybrids are quite common in regions where both cultures had influence.

Here is the name of **Primrose Hill**, which first appears in 1825 and although it most likely refers to the flower it could also be a personal name. If it is a personal name, the individual concerned is otherwise unrecorded. Fifty years earlier a record tells us of a lane named *Tinker's End* which today is known as **Tinker's Lane**. Both tell us a maker and/or seller of pots and pans was resident here.

Bestwood Park

Listings of this name are not seen until 1177 as *Beskewuda*, then in 1200 as *Beescwde*, and in 1205 as *Bescwde*. It is easy to see this as coming from the Old English *beosuc*, the first element being *beos* literally meaning 'bent grass' and describing the '(place at) the wood where bent grass grows'. Obviously grass grows vertically, though when it reaches a certain height it is no longer able to support its own weight and the wind and rain will eventually flatten it. In order for the place to be known for having 'bent grass', it must have done so for some time. Grass grows continuously, if the temperature is above 7°C, thus providing a constant source of food for grazers. The name thus tells us there were no grazing animals around here, wild or domesticated. From this we can deduce it was the first time it had been settled, while it also suggests this untapped food source was not worthwhile eating, there was an unlikely abundance of predators, or most likely was difficult to reach. While no natural obstacle is apparent today, this seems the most likely explanation and, if this reason was ever discovered, would reveal a lot about the place prior to settlement.

Bevercotes

The beaver has been extinct in England since the thirteenth century and, although there have been moves to reintroduce it to the remotest parts of Scotland, this engaging rodent is only found south of the border in place names. In 1165 the place is listed as *Beurecote*, so it is likely the beavers were still in residence at that time. The name is from two Old English words *beofor* and *cot* giving '(place at) where beavers have built their homes'. Normally the Saxon *cot* is defined as 'cottage(s)', however here the reference is certainly to the beaver's lodge. Today it is known as **Bevercotes Beck**, the ending coming from the Old Scandinavian for 'stream'. However, in a document dating from about 1289 this same stream is referred to as *Fulbek*, which comes from *ful bekkr* 'the dirty stream'. This describes a muddy stream or one with much rotting vegetation, literally 'foul' and not the most advisable source of water around.

As with many regions throughout the country there is a remoteness name attached to the most remote portion of the area. **Farleys Wood** would normally be thought to refer to a personal name, however the true origin here is 'the far woodland'.

Bilborough

Domesday's record of this place as *Bileburch* is little different from that of 1166, when it has lost that final 'h'. Doubtless this suffix is the Old English *burg* and gives us 'Bila or Billa's stronghold'.

Bilsthorpe

There is only one early record of this name, as *Bildestorp* in Domesday. As discussed in the introduction, the great eleventh-century survey has proven invaluable in revealing details about recently conquered Norman England, yet spelling accuracy of proper names simply cannot be accepted. Having said that, we can be confident that this name comes from Old Scandinavian, even fairly certain that the basis is *bildr* + *thorp*. The first element literally meant 'angle' and was used to describe the shape of an outcrop, promontory or hill. However, it was also used as a personal name, thus we are uncertain if the suffix *thorp*, meaning 'outlying farmstead', is preceded by an individual or is a topographical reference.

Locally we find minor names such as **Lockwell Hill**, which comes from Old English *loc* 'bolt, bar' and *haga* 'hedge enclosure'. This is early evidence of a hedged enclosure having a boltable gate, rather than just an opening. Today the field in question is unknown; however the hill has retained the name. **Flowers Wood** recalls the family of Thomas Flower who was resident here in 1785, while from Middle English *crifting* comes **Crifton Lodge** meaning 'the small croft or farm'.

Bingham

Listed as *Bingheham* in 1086 and *Bingeham* in 1165, this place name is from an Old English personal name together with *inga* + *ham*. Thus the name can be defined as 'the homestead of the family or followers of Bynna'. There has been suggestions that the first element may be the Saxon word *bing* meaning 'a hollow', however the element *inga* is only found after the name of an individual. Unless earlier forms are found we must assume the personal name is the correct definition.

The name of **Toot Hill** here is by no means unique. Furthermore, no matter where it is found in the land it always means the same thing, 'look out hill'.

The **Moot House** is a pub name featuring the Saxon word for a 'meeting', specifically a council or legal gathering. It is not suggested that the inn was the meeting place, simply that it was built on or near where the moot once took place. The **Wheatsheaf Inn** is a name derived from a sign. In the earliest days the sheaf would be tied to an ale stake on the road outside wherever ale was brewed. The ale stake was usually a tree where all the side branches were removed, possibly even the top cut off too, making it stand out. This is easily seen as the forerunner of the classic pub sign.

Bleasby

That Nottinghamshire stood on or near the ever-changing boundary between Saxon and Scandinavian held England is often seen in the evolution of place names. In the modern form this is evidently a Scandinavian name, which is confirmed by the record from 1256 as *Blesby* and suggesting the origin of 'Blesi's farmstead'. However, exactly three centuries earlier, in 956, this place is listed as *Blisetune*, which suggests the name was previously Saxon *tun* with the same meaning. It may be that the differences have been created by those who have recorded the names, or perhaps it is an example of a previously unknown Saxon name, or yet possibly the Saxons simply kept the name already in existence. However, if we are to accept the records as they stand, it would be nice to think this was an example of a Scandinavian individual honoured by a Saxon settlement.

Joining the Trent near here is the **Causeway Dyke**, an unusually recent name from Middle English *cauce* and derived from 'the raised way' alongside which it runs. Indeed this is a natural drainage channel running parallel to an ancient path through seasonal wetlands. We also find **Gibsmere**, a minor named derived from either 'Gippe's or Gyppi's pool', depending upon if the name is Saxon or Norse. The same confusion surrounds **Goverton**, which is either Saxon 'Godfrith's *tun*' or Norse 'Guthfrith's farmstead'.

Blidworth

When anyone has seen many pre-Norman forms of place names, Blidworth stands out as a modern name still having very Saxon overtones. Not surprisingly the early forms we have differ little from that of the twenty-first century: *Blideworde* in 1086, *Blieswurde* in 1158, *Bledwurda* in 1164 and *Bledewurda* in 1180 all point to 'the enclosure of Blitha'. The suffix is *worth* or 'enclosure', something intended to keep livestock safe overnight, rather than to deter marauding tribes.

Within the parish is the church of St Mary where, near the entrance to the churchyard, there is an unmarked grave. Traditionally this is the grave of Will Scarlet, one of Robin Hood's men and among the handful of named friends of the beloved outlaw.

Locally are a number of interesting place names, including **Fountain Dale** which has only been known as such since 1826. Prior to this the name was recorded as *Langton* or 'the long settlement', a reference to its shape. The present name has no known etymology and there is unlikely to have been any, the name being simply chosen. However, the reason for it being selected and why a change of name was considered are not recorded.

Stone at Bleasby marking the site of an ancient cross, erected by donation in 2000.

Rainworth comes from Old Scandinavian. However, it is unclear from the known records if this comes from *hreinn vrath* 'the clean ford' or *rein vrath* 'the boundary strip by the ford'. **Python Hill** has nothing to do with snakes, it is a corruption of *Pythorn* as recorded on a map of 1826. This features an old abbreviation for one of Britain's most conspicuous birds and speaks of 'a hill with a thorn bush where magpies are seen'.

The name of **Fishpool** seems a little odd, for there is no sign of there ever having been a pond here. Indeed we would normally expect to find this name as Fishpond, corruptions of such a name are extremely rare. A record from 1609 may offer the answer, for it gives this as *fishpole feld*. This would seem a more likely explanation as being where trees were pollarded in order to produce poles for fishing. This is probably not a reference to a hand-held pole, for supply would have far outweighed demand, but used as stakes which were driven into the bed of the river. Placed close together they would have allowed the smaller fish to pass through, while funnelling the larger food fish into wicker baskets from which they could not escape and made them easy to collect.

There is also a **Providence Farm**, which does mean what it seems. It is unusual to find a name praising the land. As has already been said, names are usually coined by others, not by those in residence. Neighbours are, by nature, more likely to be critical than to praise, hence this name was almost certainly given by the owners.

Three local inns here, all with different origins. Public houses have ever been associated with sports and games; it takes little imagination to see the **Fox and Hounds** was the start/finish of the hunt. Coloured animal names are normally an indication of an heraldic origin, however the **Black Bull** is probably a simple reference to an agricultural region and the colour made it simpler to show on the sign – a major consideration where money is concerned.

Lastly is the name of the **The Bird in Hand**, which instantly brings to mind 'A bird in the hand is worth two in the bush' and a saying which is thought to date from at least pre-Roman times. Clearly, the suggestion that what you could ever desire would be found within is an advertising ploy. Sign painters throughout history have found increasingly subtle and imaginative ways of depicting this name.

Blyth

A place which has taken its name from the river on which it stands. Old English *blithe* meant 'the gentle, or pleasant one', clearly a reference to the current. As a river name it is almost certainly the most popular of Saxon origins, with examples also found in Northumberland, the West Midlands, Suffolk and Staffordshire.

Blyth Hill Law refers to a tumulus found west of the ancient road from Nottingham to Blyth. **Briber Hill** is another 'hill' name, this time a reference to 'the hill by Blyth', although it is uncertain if this means the river or the settlement. From the Old English *bi northan ea* comes the modern **Nornay**, which means '(place) north of the water' and is in reference to the River Ryton.

Welcome to Blyth!

Since the first inns and taverns, there has been a connection between them and religious establishments. Often they were the only two places in the community which actively welcomed strangers, while they were naturally the commonest meeting places. Thus there was a degree of inevitability of the names being connected. Indeed, there are a surprising number of pub names which have religious origins as we shall see elsewhere in the book. Here the name of the **Angel** has obvious religious connections, yet that it is so common is simply because it is such a simple sign to produce and instantly recognisable.

Bole

Domesday records this place as *Bolun*, which comes from either Old English *bola* or Old Scandinavian *bolr*, although both have identical meanings. In fact the modern name means exactly the same thing, suggesting the 'bole' or main trunk of the tree. Here the word is used to infer the settlement could be found 'within the tree trunks'. This might seem to be a simple reference to a woodland clearing, yet it is probably more literal in that the trunks were simply just trunks – i.e. they had been pollarded to encourage the growth of straight new poles ideal for use as building material.

There is a **Bole Field Farm** here and records of this place go back some time. Perhaps this was the site of the original farm which gave its name to the place, rather than the reverse.

Bothamsall

From listings such as *Bodmescel* in 1086, *Bodmeshil* in 1211, *Botmeshil* in 1212, and *Bothmeshill* in 1213, we can see this name comes from two Saxon or Old English words *bothm* and *scelf*. This is therefore the '(place at) the shelf of land by a broad river valley', a highly descriptive name which gives a reasonable snapshot of the region in Saxon times.

Locally are two quite unusual names, even for England, which merit some attention. The name of **Spitfire Bottoms**, for example, may conjure up images of the most famous of fighter aircraft but the true origin is more simple. The second part of the name is fairly self-explanatory, the region is at the bottom of a slope. This slope affords a natural updraft which, in a time when bellows were man-powered, provided an effective flow of air to fuel a kiln(s) or furnace(s). Clearly such would have been running continuously and, looking up, the residents would have seen the light from the crest of the ridge appear to 'spit fire'.

Secondly is the name of **Conjure Alders**, a much corrupted name which has only comparatively recently gained the 'Alders' referring to the trees here. Additions such as these are normally only found added to common names to distinguish them from each other. However, Conjure is hardly a common name, indeed it is almost certainly unique and hardly warrants any distinctive addition. It seems most likely the addition evolved as the first element does not stand alone well. So where does this unique 'Conjure' originate? The name comes from a corruption of the Old Scandinavian *konungr-vath* or 'the king's ford'. The ford in question is an ancient crossing point and would have been here before the Romans arrived, not simply the Norsemen who named it. It carries the Nottingham to Blyth road across the River Maun at a point just below its confluence with the Meden. It is quite possible that the earlier name has influenced the pronunciation and thus the evolution of the name.

Boughton

A fairly common place name and one which has four distinct origins. This should not be confused with names which have alternative meanings, for here there are three certain and quite different origins which have all evolved to become Broughton.

Generally speaking the origin depends on the location. Those in Kent, for example, refer to 'the farmstead by beech trees', while in the counties of the

Midlands the first element could be a personal name, or Old English *bucc* or *bucca* – 'stags' and 'male goats' respectively.

The name of Boughton in Nottinghamshire was recorded in Domesday as *Buchetone* and a few years later as *Buketon*. While the evidence is sparse, the forms are enough to show the most likely origin here is the personal name and is 'Bucca's farmstead'. The alternatives of stags and he-goats should not be completely discounted, yet those elements do not easily lend themselves to the records we have.

Among the local names found here are **Birkhill Wood**, where the modern addition is virtually the same as the original 'hill where birch grows'. **Whinny Lane** runs past **Whinny Hill** from where it gets its name, the element common to both means 'covered with gorse'. Of course there is also the often found 'remoteness' name, here being **New Zealand Cottages**.

The local is the **Carpenters Arms**. Originally featuring the coat of arms of this ancient trade, it suggests the owner or landlord of this place was previously employed in that trade.

Bradmore

It may seem fairly obvious that the suffix refers to moorland. However, early forms, such as *Brademere* and *Brademar* from 1086 and 1226 respectively, show it to be something quite different. The true Saxon origin here is *brad mere* '(place at) the broad pool'.

This is another of those names which give a glimpse into life in centuries past. Today there is no broad pool, lake, or pond here. Presumably it was drained for agricultural purposes.

Bramcote

From early forms such as *Broncote* and *Brunecote* from the eleventh century, to the modern form recorded as early as 1197, all point to the same origin. This comes from the Old English *brom cot*, 'the cottages where broom grows'.

The name of **Codling's Yard** appears on maps from 1840, a reference to former resident Samuel Codling who was living here at that time.

The rose is by far the most popular flower featured in pub names and signs. The majority of the older signs show allegiance to the monarchy. In more recent times a succession of names have included the name of the rose. At Bramcote the name is **The Rose Grower**, although there are no more roses here than anywhere else so it must refer to a former landlord. Also here is **The Sherwin Arms**, named after a Nottinghamshire family who served the community for many years, including several terms as mayor of the city of Nottingham.

Brinsley

With earliest listings such as *Brunesleia* 1086, *Brynesley* 1185, and *Brunnesleye* 1198, the suffix here is Old English *leah* or 'woodland clearing'. The first element is likely a personal name, either Bryn or Brun. Indeed, a record from before the Norman Conquest mentions a man named Brun holding four bovates of land here. A bovate is not an exact measure of land, being an approximation of the amount of land ploughed by oxen in a year, but could be said to be around 6 hectares.

To say the name of Brun mentioned is the person who gave his name to Brinsley is certainly tempting, for it would be almost unique to be able to cite the individual who gave their name to a place, especially when that person was not of noble birth. However, we could suggest that the person mentioned as holding land here was named after the original Brun who may well have been an ancestor.

Three pubs here recall both local history and that of the county, the latter seen in the name of the **Robin Hood Inn**. Now it is quite likely that the stories told are, at best, an exaggeration. However, pubs named Robin Hood are found throughout the country, even though most are actually renamed from the Ancient Order of Foresters, the only connection being the famed outfit of green. It is no surprise to find the name of Nottinghamshire's most famous figure on the sign in Brinsley.

The White Lion is heraldic, normally found to be taken from the coat of arms of Edward IV, the Dukes of Norfolk, or the Earls of March. Then there is **The Yew Tree**, which doubtless took its name from this long-living tree which grew close to the establishment.

Brough

A name found a few times around the north and Midlands, always from Old English *burh* and meaning 'stronghold, fortified place'. Oddly the place is not recorded in this county before 1525, rather late for a name of Saxon origins. It seems safe to assume that, while the place was not recorded, locally it had always been known by this name since its occupation in a much earlier age.

Budby

Unlike some names there is no doubt the first element here is an Old Scandinavian personal name together with *by*. Records exist of *Butebi* and *Buttebi*, from 1086 and 1169 respectively, meaning 'Butti's farmstead'.

There are several local names of interest here. **Perlethorpe** tells us it was once a 'dependent settlement' and must have been not only a separate place once but probably an overspill site. **Hanger Hill** might conjure up images of felons hanging from gallows, yet it is actually the point where three adjoining parishes meet and is 'the hill of the assembly or meeting'.

Old Scandinavian *lundr* or 'wood' follows the personal name Authr, and has evolved to become **Osland Wood**. Another wood is named from its shape, although it is difficult to see the likeness in **Cocked Hat Wood** today. Former resident William Pickin and his family, who were here in 1790, have given their name to **Pickin's Bridge**. Similarly, **Duncan Wood** and **Vincent Grove** were name after Viscount Duncan and Earl St Vincent respectively.

Bulcote

Records of this name include *Bulecote* in 1086 and in the modern form as early as 1242. The literal translation is 'the bull's cottages'. However, this should be seen as 'sheds' rather than cottages.

Bulwell

Once again there is some confusion as to whether the first element is a personal name or not. Listings as *Buleuuelle*, *Bulwelle* and *Bulewell*, in 1086, 1165 and 1169 respectively, point to either Old English *bula* + *wella* 'the spring or stream where bulls drink', although perhaps the first element is the name Bula.

The name of **Rise Farm** is easy to misunderstand. Its beginnings have nothing to do with the lie of the land but come from Old English *hris* referring to the 'brushwood' in this area when it was first farmed. **Snape Wood** is also from the Saxon tongue. Here the basis is *snaepe* meaning 'boggy land'.

One local has a unique name which reflects the culture of the county perfectly. **The Framesmiths Arms** remembers the craftsmen who built the frames which were used for many years in the hosiery and lace industries, both well known Nottinghamshire products. **The Limekiln** was so named because it stood near where limestone was burned in kilns to produce lime, used in both building and agriculture since pre-history.

The **Lion Revived** is one of the most unusual names. It stands on the site of the former White Lion which also explains the etymology. The Royal Scots Greys took their name from the grey horses they rode. Part of this regiment were stationed in Bulwell during the riots of 1840, and **The Scots Grey** public house was named for this reason.

Bunny

A name which would probably figure high on a list of Nottinghamshire's favourite place names. However, it would probably be much less popular if we all spoke fluent Old

The church at Bunny.

English and could see this was simply 'dry ground in a marsh where reeds grow', from *bune* + *eg*. Some sources suggest the stream here was once known as the Bune. If this is correct then the stream also took its name from the reeds which must have proliferated there.

The **Rancliffe Arms** recalls the Parkyns family who were resident in Bunny since at least the seventeenth century. The title Baron Rancliffe is a currently dormant peerage of Ireland.

Burton Joyce

Burton is one of the most popular names in England, although not all have the same origins. As such these are often found with a defining addition. This place has its origins in Old English *byrh* + *tun*, 'the farmstead of the fortified place'.

Records of this name include *Bertone* in 1086, *Birtun* in 1236, and *Birton Jorce* in 1348. This last form is the first record of the de Jorz family, lords of the manor from at least the thirteenth century.

Minor place names here include the delightfully named **Crock Dumble**, describing 'the crooked, wooded valley with a stream'. Nearby **Stockhill Farm** was founded on 'the stump hill' although it will never be known if the trees were cleared to provide farmland or if the farm was sited here because the stumps were all that remained.

C

Calverton

Domesday's record of *Caluretone* shows this to be from the Old English *calfra* + *tun*, meaning 'the farmstead where calves are reared'. This Saxon name tells us more of the history of Calverton than would first be apparent. Firstly, we can deduce that the pasture must have been of consistently good quality, for cattle require a higher quality grass than sheep or goats to thrive. Secondly, cattle must have been raised here for some time to become well known as a place specialising in cattle.

Occasionally defining the name of a place can produce a mental image of life in Saxon times. To my mind these names are worth taking the time to define and to savour.

Even earlier, before the Romans arrived, the Celtic peoples had created a network of trackways across a predominantly woodland Britain. The original need for these routes was purely for trade, in particular salt. There can be few towns in the land which does not have some reference to these former saltways. At Calverton we find 'the ford of the salters', today marked on the map as **Salterford Farm**.

Carburton

A name which has proven difficult to define and, while any certain definition may still evade us, perhaps we can suggest an alternative or two.

The name is listed in Domesday as *Carbertone*, in 1169 as *Karberton*, and in 1174 as *Carberton*. Because Burton is such as common place name, from *bere-tun* and meaning 'barley farm', this has been accepted as the ending which left the first syllable Car- without any plausible basis.

However, perhaps looking at if from another angle might help to solve this puzzle. There is an Old English word *carr* meaning 'hill', and the hill nearby is quite evident even today. If the term was to describe this as a 'rocky hill' then we might expect the name to be *Carrbeorg* and then this place becomes *Carrbeorg-tun* or 'the farmstead near the hill called Carrbeorg'. This cannot be offered as the derivation without further evidence. However it does show that, with a little creative thinking, a quite plausible origin can be found which might just point the next generation of researchers in the right direction.

A wealth of interesting names are found in this parish, including two remoteness names – both of which are very relevant, for **Scotland** is in the extreme north, while **Gibraltar** is not only in a far corner but forms a similar isthmus shape. Here is **Thompson's Covert**, named after former resident Joseph Thompson who was here in 1774. However, **Mellish's Plantation** cannot be tied down to a specific individual. This must be simply because it has not been recorded as the surname Mellish is common to this region; indeed it may well have started here.

Another minor name tied to this area features an element found only around Nottinghamshire, Lincolnshire and Yorkshire. **Long Valley Screed** is obvious except for the last word which is an old dialect term meaning 'parcel of land'. We also find the names **Pitiful Hill** and **Pitiful Wood**, both coined as derogatory names for a region which probably provided poor return for its farmers.

Two pubs here merit a mention. The **Cherry Tree** would have once been named for a prominent or well-known tree of this variety which stood close by. **The Admiral Rodney** recalls George Brydges, Lord Rodney (1719–92) whose distinguished naval career is best remembered for one battle. In 1782 he was victorious over the French at the Battle of the Saintes, fought in the West Indies. It sent ripples through the political halls of the day, drawing attention to a potentially volatile situation and culminating in a stronger peace with the French following the American Revolution.

Car Colston

This is an Old English name listed as *Colestone* in 1086, *Kyrcoluiston* in 1242, and *Kercolston* in 1271. The earlier forms show this to be derived from 'Kolr's farmstead', with the additional first element describing 'a marsh'. However, there are signs of Scandinavian influence during the thirteenth century, and that the name came from the Old Norse *kirkja*, which had nothing to do with the name but was a misunderstanding by those recording the name.

One local name is **Shackerdale Farm**, which has an interesting origin. The farm is named from the region of Shackerdale which comes from two Old English words *sceacere* 'robber' and *dael* 'valley'. It seems highly improbable that this was where felons lived, while to suggest it was the scene of a robbery or a well-known location for robberies also seems implausible. The only reasonable answer is it refers to the land, perhaps where crops were in danger of being ruined by unseasonal flooding or ownership taken by another person under questionable circumstances.

Carlton

A quite common place name, found particularly in several northern English counties. Domesday's *Karletun* and *Carleton* in 1242, the origins are Old English *ceorl* + *tun*, 'the farmstead of the freement or peasants'. It should be noted that Domesday's entry may well show Scandinavian influence from *karl*, although the meaning is the same.

The name of **Standhill**, while often said to be 'the stony hill', is simply a corrupted version of *standell* which refers to 'the place of the quarry'. However, the name of **Thorneywood** is quite obviously what it says, '(the place at) the thorny wood'. To the experienced eye, the name of **Marshall Hill Farm** features at least two elements which do not fit together and thus are almost certainly taken from a personal name. Indeed, a record from 1294 shows it to have been associated with one Walter le Mareschall. The personal name is, as with many family names, from a place name and tells us of 'the marshy corner of land'. A marsh on a hill would be highly unusual, the slope would have allowed the region to drain, thus Marshall Hill is almost certainly a family name.

The more common place names often have an additional second name to differentiate them from the rest. In Nottingham there is also a **Carlton on Trent**, also recorded in Domesday but as *Carletune*. Clearly the addition refers to the county's major river, the name of which is discussed under its own entry.

Joining the Trent at Carlton is a small tributary known simply as **The Beck**. This is derived from the Old Scandinavian *bekkr* meaning 'stream'. Above the settlement stands **Crossley Hill**, a name which probably belonged to a place at the foot of the hill rather than the hill itself. This features the Old English element *leah* or 'woodland clearing'. The first element may have referred to the cross-like shape of the clearing, or maybe there was a cross here. If the latter is the case it would almost certainly have been a way marker and would not have held any religious significance.

The unsually named **Swine Plex** features an obvious first element and a very usual second part. This is of Middle English origins and can be defined as 'small plot of land where pigs are seen'. These would have been domesticated animals, not wild hogs. The family of Mr Cowlishaw, here in 1776, gave their name to **Cowlishaw Plantation**, although no individuals are specifically named in either of the known documents.

Costhorpe is a simple enough name to define yet it is highly unusual for it features a known individual. Although earlier records are rather vague, it seems certain that the place was simply known as *Thorpe* since the days of the Scandinavian influence and a common enough word meaning 'outlying farmstead'. However, a document from 1195 states how these lands were taken by the king and said to be called *Cossardtorp*, which is easy to see as an early form of Costhorpe. However, history also records significant events in the previous year. Lord of the manor, Ralf Coshart, had rebelled against Richard I. His rebellion was quickly subdued and his holdings taken by the Crown.

Local inns have some interesting and unusual names. **The Windsor Castle** is an indirect reference to the monarchy, while enabling the sign painter the easy task of reproducing the simple and easily recognised shape of the royal residence. The **Elwes Arms** recalls the family who were Lord Lieutenants of England and Wales. **Inn for a Penny** is an attempt at humour in the hope it will attract custom. Finally there is a pub which was once known as the **Old Contemptible**. The British Expeditionary Force fought at Mons in 1914 and it is said they gained their nickname when the Kaiser referred to them as 'General French's contemptible little army'. The pub at Carlton had a sign depicting a man in the uniform of a First World War soldier. It was decided to change the name of the pub and, while the landlord was on annual leave, the brewery changed the sign. The **Old Volunteer** shows the soldier working his way through a huge pile of potatoes armed with only a potato peeler, obviously as some form of punishment. The landlord's comments upon his return were not recorded.

Caunton

Despite the plethora of early forms such as *Calnestune*, *Calmodeston*, *Kalnadatun*, and *Calfnadtun* – these were recorded over a period of less than eighty years – the personal which forms the first element is still uncertain. This is most likely due to it being an uncommon name, or a pet form of a name, or even a nickname.

We can be sure that the suffix is Old English or Saxon *tun* and can suggest an origin of something not unlike 'the farmstead of a man called Calnoth'.

Local names include **Earlshaw House** which features the element *haga* and speaks of 'the enclosure of the earl', meaning it was on land held by whomever was in that office. However, the name of **Knapthorpe**, which comes from the Old English *cnapa thorpe* meaning 'boy's outlying farmstead', is not a true name or even a description but a nickname. The individual concerned would have either led the settlement at an early age or, more likely, looked younger than he was and had boyish features. The name of **Newbottles Plantation**, listed as *Neubo* in the thirteenth century, comes from Old English *botl* and means 'the place of the new building'.

Caythorpe

In 1177 this place is found as *Cathorp* and two years later as *Catthorp*. This is from an Old Scandinavian personal name with *thorp* giving us 'Kati's outlying farmstead'.

Chilwell

Domesday's listings as *Cilleuuelle* and *Ciduuelle*, although the record from 1194 as *Childewella* is closer to the original Saxon name for this place. From Old English *cild* + *wella* this is 'the spring or stream where young people gather'.

This definition leads us to ask why anyone would be gathering here, what was the attraction? We may be looking at the meaning too literally. Perhaps the 'children' referred to are in fact water sprites, and the place was considered to be an early religious site. Without further evidence it seems the reference will probably remain a mystery.

The local name of **Attenborough**, a famous personal name, is derived from another personal name and tells us this was once 'Adda's fortified place'. **Cop Hill** was named after another person, one Roger de Coppewell who was here in 1333, although the modern place name is not found until 1826.

Cobbed Spring is taken from Old English meaning 'hill spring' from the word *coppe* meaning literally 'top'.

The local pub is **The Cadland Inn**. It refers to the racehorse owned by the Duke of Rutland. In the Epsom Derby of 1828 it ran against The Colonel, both horses being declared winners in a dead heat. As was the norm at the time, the race was re-run and Cadland won by a neck.

Clarborough

Most names are descriptive, some much more so than others. Indeed, some names can be seen almost as snapshots of the Saxon era. Clarborough is one such name. Listed as *Claureburg* in 1086, *Clauerburg* in 1185, and *Clareburg* in 1242, there is no doubt this is from Old English *claefre + burg*. Such a combination is very unusual, possibly unique, yet this is certainly 'the fortification overgrown by clover'.

Names here include **Welham**, telling us there was a 'homestead at the springs' founded some time before the Norman Conquest. Later, **Clarborough Hill Farm** was the home of Thomes del Hull who was here in 1327. By 1850 Henry Hutchinson's family had given their name to **Hutchinson's Holt**. However, **Whinleys House** took its name from the location, itself from Saxon *whin leys* or 'where gorse grows near pasture'.

Clayworth

No shortage of early records for this name, including *Clavorde* in 1086, *Claworth* in 1130, *Clawurda* in 1156, *Clauewurda* in 1164, and *Clauwurda* in 1177. This is 'the enclosure on or by the low curving hill' and comes from Old English *clawu + worth*.

While the name of **Black Syke Drain** is easier to see as the 'dark small stream used as a drain', other names may be harder to define were it not for the excellent records kept by parishes throughout history. **Royston Manor** was the home of the Royston family by 1676, Roger Otter was in residence near **Otter's Bridge** in 1682, and Samuel Grey had set up home close to **Gray's Bridge** some time before 1850.

St Peter's church,
Clayworth.

Clifton

One of the most commonly found place names in England, often found in combination with another name to differentiate it from the others. All of the examples are from Old English *clif* + *tun* and meaning 'the farmstead by the cliff or bank'.

California Farm is one of those minor place names which, although seemingly named in honour of a far-flung corner of the planet, is actually an attempt at humorously describing the farthest outpost of the parish. The same is not the case with **Rome Farm**, although the Italian capital city may well have influenced the evolution. Here the origin is Old Scandinavian *rum* meaning 'space'.

Here we also find **Glapton**, a name of Old English or Saxon origin meaning 'Glappa's *tun* or farmstead'. **Butler's Barn** takes its name from former resident Ellen Butler, who is documented as being here by 1576.

The **Crusader** was named after the twelfth-century squire, Sir Gervase Clifton. He was killed fighting on the Third Crusade and friends and colleagues brought his heart back in a casket which still resides in the local church. The **Grey Mare** is a name which likely commemorates a favoured animal, possibly belonging to a landlord or owner, which may well have belonged to them before they came to Clifton.

Clipston

Listed in Domesday as *Cliston* and as *Clipstun* in 1236, this is an example of a Scandinavian and Saxon hybrid place name. Here the Old English *tun* is the suffix, with the name meaning 'the farmstead of Klyppr or Klippr'.

Clipstone

Despite the similarity with the previous name and the identical meaning, the record in Domesday is markedly different as *Clipestune*. However, this is still 'the farmstead of either Klyppr or Klippr'.

There is a lost settlement here, although the addition to the basic name makes **Clipstone Shroggs** worth a mention. This addition features a word common only to Nottinghamshire and Yorkshire, where *shroggs* is used to describe 'bushes, underbrush'. This was particularly appropriate as this place was at the western boundary of Clipstone Forest.

Here is a tributary of the Maun, **Vicar Water**, clearly named from land held by the church. Furthermore, this most likely started off as a local nickname. Records show this is a very recent name, not known before 1826. Previously it was known as *Warmebroke* (1450), a name which says exactly what it means, 'the warm brook'.

Lindley's Plantation recalls the tenancy of John Lindley, who was around here by 1840. There is also **Parliament Oak**, said to be where a 'parliament' or meeting was held during the time of King John. However, the name is not recorded before 1826, thus it may well be a local legend and is open to debate whether this was a meeting place during the early thirteenth century.

The local inn is **The Dog and Duck** which, apart from being an example of aliteration and much favoured by advertisers, is also a reminder of an ancient pastime. Pubs such as this were near the village pond and remember the duck hunting as it was. Favoured by Charles II, ducks were released on to the pond with their wings pinned, thus their only means of escape from the pursuing spaniels was to dive.

Coddington

Records of this name include *Cotintone* in 1086, *Chodingtona* in 1163, *Gotingt* in 1185, and *Cotingdon* in 1280. Clearly whoever recorded the name in the late twelfth century had little knowledge of Saxon place names, for there can be little doubt this is 'the farm of the people of Codda (or maybe Cotta)'.

Locally we find **Moor Brats**, the second element from Old English *braec* and telling us this was 'land newly set aside for cultivation on the moor'. We also find **Tinderbox** which, owing to the children's tale of that name, may lead us to think of an origin quite different than the true meaning. This is a derogatory term, one of contempt suggesting it was good for firewood and little else.

Collingham

Over the space of less than a century there are no less than four different forms recorded – as *Colingeham* in 1194, *Colingham* in 1270, and *Northcolingham* and *Southcolingham* in 1291. These last two examples suggest the settlement had become somewhat scattered. An Old English personal name + *inga* + *ham* leads us to the defining this name as 'the homestead of the family or followers of Col (or Cola)'.

The north of Collingham has the local name of **Danethorpe Hill**. This is obviously a name where the place has given its name to the local hill; any earlier name for the hill is unknown. Here is a place name of Saxon origin 'Deormund's outlying farmstead'. **Cow Wath Pool** has two self-explanatory elements around the Old Scandinavian *vath* or 'ford', while **Mons Pool** comes from former resident Henry Mons who was here by 1366.

The southern part of the village has a **Trow Bridge**, which can still be seen as the Old English 'tree bridge' although it this suggests a log across a stream when it is more likely to have been 'wooden bridge'.

Colston

There are two places with this name in Nottinghamshire, separated by a distance of about 5 miles. This is another example of a hybrid name, a Scandinavian personal name with the Old English *tun*, giving us 'the farmstead of Kolr'.

Car Colston is listed as *Colestone* in 1086 and *Kyrcoluiston* in 1242. The addition is also Scandinavian, from *kirkja* meaning 'church'. **Colston Bassett** is recorded quite separately in Domesday as *Coletone* and as *Coleston Bassett* in 1228. Here the addition is a manorial one, referring to the family who were at the helm from at least the twelfth century.

Colwick

Records of this name over the centuries include *Colui* in 1086, *Collewich* in 1211, *Colwyk* in 1302, and *Collick* in 1680. This suffix is Old English *wic* meaning 'specialised farm' and here, as with the vast majority of cases, is understood to be 'Cola's dairy farm'.

The Starting Gate is a name found throughout the land always near to a racecourse, or where racehorses are stabled or trained. Clearly the sign depicts the gate used before the starting stalls, although it is still used at certain meetings and courses.

Cossall

A name of Old English derivation, this was originally the '(place at) the nook of land associated with Cott'. The personal name here is followed by *halh*, which is often seen in modern place names as the element 'hall'. Cossall place is found in records as *Coteshale* in 1086, *Cozale* in 1200, and *Cozhall* in 1242.

Costock

Listings such as *Cortingestoche* in 1086, *Cortingestoce* in 1100, *Curtlingestoke* in 1211, *Chirtlingastoca* in 1158, and *Kortincstok* in 1236 leave this Old English name in no doubt. From a Saxon personal name + *inga* + *stoc* this place was 'the specialised farmstead of the family or followers of Cort'. Invariably the 'specialised farm' referred to a dairy farm, although it could also have produced honey, eels, leather, or any other desired commodity.

Cotgrave

With a suffix from Old English *graf*, this place name is derived from '(place at) the grove or copse of a man called Corta'. Listings of this place include *Godegrave* in 1086, *Cotegrava* in 1094, *Cottegraua* in 1158, and *Cotesgava* in 1316.

Thurlbeck Dyke is the local stream, a name which comes from Old Scandinavian 'Thorleif's stream'. **Candleby Lane** is named after a man who brought his family here from Candleby in Lincolnshire. **The Gripps**, which means a 'small drain', comes from a dialect word *grip* and is thus a very localised name. **Stragglethorpe** has two elements, the latter referring to an outlying farm while the first, today used to mean lagging behind, had this same meaning here but is describing farming techniques which are 'old fashioned', particularly if they were unsuccessful.

Risegate Lane refers to the 'brushwood road', and would have run alongside rather than to it. **Brookhill Plantation** features the Saxon term *broc*, still used as an alternative name for these islands' largest carnivore for this is 'the hole where badgers are seen'. Other residents of Cotgrave are remembered in **Scrotton's Hill**, **Smart's Hill** and **Thorton's Holt**, recalling residents William Scrottern who was here in 1729, William Smart here in 1799, and Henry Thornton here in 1850.

Cotham

As *Cotune* in Domesday, *Cotes* in 1197, and *Cotum* in 1264, the name is from an Old English *cotum* itself the plural of *cot* or cottage. Indeed, this is the meaning 'the place of the cottages'.

Nearby, the **Back Dyke** joins the Trent. This river name is derived from the Old Scandinavian *bekkr* meaning simply 'stream'. We also find the name of **Booth's Buildings** on the maps of this place, referring to land held by John Booth in 1850.

Cottam

Listed as *Cotum* in 1274, this place has identical beginnings to that of the previous entry, Cotham, and is 'the place of the cottages'.

While they would have hoped to have left a more glamorous legacy, the Seymour family have only given their name to the drainage channel of **Seymour Drain**; yet without it the land would probably have been too wet and crops would have rotted in the ground. Another name, that of **North Brecks,** takes its name from the 'cultivated land', literally 'broken ground'. The additional 'North' is to distinguish it from Westbrecks in nearby South Leverton, just 4 miles south-east of here.

Cromwell

Quite likely the place gave its name to the ancestors of the former Lord Protector of England, Oliver Cromwell. However the place name existed well before then, records of *Crunwelle* in 1086, *Crumwella* in 1186, and *Crumbwell* in 1230 prove this. The origins here are Old English or Saxon *crumb + wella*, with the first element literally meaning 'crooked'. This conveys a message of '(the place at) the winding stream'.

Cropwell

Two places of this name separated by less than a mile have each acquired a second element to distinguish between the two. The basic name comes from Old English *crop* + *hyll* 'the rounded hill'. Almost certainly the feature was known by this name well before any settlements arrived.

Records of these places are found as *Crophille* in 1086, *Croppill Boteiller* in 1265, and *Bischopcroppehill* in 1280. **Cropwell Bishop** refers to it being held by the Archbishop of York while to the north **Cropwell Butler** was held by the Butler family from at least the twelfth century.

Cuckney

There are a number of listings of this place which show varying spellings of the original form; *Cuchenai* in 1086, *Chugeneia* in 1185, *Quikenea* in 1195, *Cokenenye* in 1211, and *Coknay* in 1510, the modern form not seen until 1684. This suffix is from Saxon *eg*, giving a definition of 'Cuca or Cwica's dry land in marsh'. It may seem that the alternative personal names are quite dissimilar, yet the pronunciation of each is not much different. Without other, earlier forms, it is impossible to be more precise.

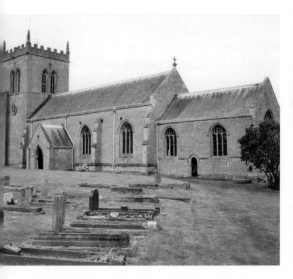

Above, left: *St Mary's parish church, Cuckney.*

Above, right: *A beautifully landscaped pond and waterfall near Cuckney.*

D

Darlton

Records such as *Derluuetun*, *Derlintun* and *Derleton*, in 1086, 1156 and 1172 respectively, show this to be a rare, but not unique, example of a place name based on that of a female personal name. With the suffix from the Old English *tun* this is 'the farmstead of a woman called Deorlufu'.

Three local names attract our interest here. **Kingshaugh Close** is named from the field which was told to us was 'the king's *haga* or enclosure'. As with many parishes, Darlton has given a remoteness name to its farthest corner. However, it is somewhat unusual to find the name **America**. Lastly is **Honeywell**, which was listed in 1606 as *Hony hole feild* and shows the origin to be 'muddy hole' – a somewhat less sweet sounding term than the modern form.

Daybrook

Originally the name of a small tributary of the Leen, it has also become a district of the county town. The first element here has become somewhat corrupted, the true meaning is 'the deep brook'. While it has never been particularly deep in any sense that we would recognise, the width compared to the depth is notable.

Devon

Not the county but a river. Indeed, although the names are identical they have just about as diverse origins as is possible – the county is named after the Celtic tribe which lived there, the Dumnonni. While it is known that this major tributary of the Trent has its origins in the same Celtic tongue, it is not certain if the basis is *dubno* or *dubo* for both are quite apt. Running in a steep ravine it could refer to 'deep' from *dubno*, or the same topography gives the river a dark appearance which could be *dubo* or 'black'.

Drayton

This is a common place name, indeed there are two in Nottingham with obvious differences, **East Drayton** and **West Drayton**. Listed as *Draitone* and *Draitun* in 1086, *Est Draiton* in 1276, and *West Draytone* in 1269, these places are no different from every other Drayton in the country. From Old English *draeg + tun* this refers to 'the farmstead at or near a portage'. A portage could be a number of things. However, all involve dragging something over a short distance in order to take advantage of a possible shortcut. This could be a marshland between two navigable stretches of water, or perhaps a slope where goods were winched up from a dock.

At East Drayton is found **Dolegate Road**, a name which comes from Old Scandinavian *dal gata* meaning 'road to the portion of land'. Meanwhile at West Drayton is **Merriall Bridge**, from *myrig hielde* telling of 'the bridge by a pleasant slope'. However, this was not always the name, for there is an earlier record of *Eelpie Bridge*. The name came from Eel Pye House nearby which, in 1775, was an eating house on the Great North Road.

Dunham

A name found four times in England, all coming from Old English *dun + ham* 'the homestead at the hill'. Domesday lists the place as *Duneham*, however the modern form appears as early as 1157. Local names include **Chequers Lane**, which ran alongside the former *Chequer Pasture* in 1632 and was named for its obvious chequered appearance.

E

Eakring

An unusual sound to this, for a place name, due to it being wholly of Scandinavian origin. Listed as *Ecringhe*, *Echeringhe*, *Aichringa*, and *Aikering* from the late eleventh to the early thirteenth centuries, this comes from *eik* + *hringr*, giving the '(place at) the ring of oak trees'. Although there is no evidence to show the settlement was within the circle, it seems unlikely to have been elsewhere.

Among the minor names here is **Eakring Brail Wood**, the middle element coming from *braec*. This word has been known from Romano-British times and can only be understood by association with other languages, in particular the Dutch evolution of *briel*, *briul*, *broel*, *brogel* which point to a definition of 'land recently set aside for cultivation'. There is also the name of **Dumble**, which is a Middle English word meaning 'pit' or 'pool'.

East Bridgford

A name which has the addition to distinguish it from West Bridgford. Records of this name go back to Domesday and *Brugeforde* in 1086, *Brigeford* in 1149, *Briggeford* in 1284, and *Brygeforthe on Hyll* in 1558. Logically, the ford was here before the bridge and there would have been a period when both were in existence, although the age of these names tell us the bridge must have replaced the earlier crossing a very long time ago.

Individuals who have left their influence on this place in the names found on maps and in the landscape include Gabriel Brunts who was here in 1590 and is remembered by **Brunt's Lane**. In 1631 Edmund Watson was working land now known as **Watson's Piece**, while in 1850 Thomas Straw was living and working along **Straw's Lane**.

Eastwood

Early records of this name are found as *Estewic* in 1086, *Estweit* in 1165, *Est Twait* in 1166, and *Estthwet* in 1185. This name comes from two elements from different languages, Old English *east* and Old Scandinavian *thveit*, giving 'the east clearing'. As has already been said, the names of our places are coined by the neighbours. Here it is fairly obvious that Eastwood was most likely named by the inhabitants of Heanor.

Locally we find **Cocker House** built on land where poultry was reared and which gave the name to 'the cock enclosure'.

Pubs around Eastwood include the **Man In Space**. Built in 1966 the sign shows an astronaut weightless in space at the end of a line. It shows a landmark moment in the space race with the somewhat erroneously named 'space walk'. The **Palmerston Arms** recalls Henry John Temple, 3rd Viscount Palmerston, English statesman who served two terms as prime minister.

Eaton

One of the most common place names in the country, most derived from Old English *ea* + *tun* 'the farmstead by a river', hardly surprising that it is so common with such a simple beginning. A reliable and local water supply was as much a necessity for the Saxon farm as it is for their twenty-first-century counterparts.

Edingley

Another Saxon name, with the common Old English elements *inga* + *leah*. The listing from 1291 of *Eddyngley* seems only vaguely similar and yet, just eleven years later, the modern spelling is found. The evolution of this name to the modern form is exactly as we would expect, for this place was originally 'the place in the woodland clearing of the family or followers of Eddi'.

The only watercourse of note is recorded as *la Becke* in 1584. From Old Scandinavian *bekkr* it means simply 'stream'. Later it took on the name of the place to differentiate it from every other 'beck' in the area.

Minor place names in and around Edingley include **Wolfeleyhill Farm**. From Old English *wulfa hlaw* and meaning 'wolves burial mound or hill', this more likely refers to a local legend (maybe even a person nicknamed 'Wolf') than being a place where any wolf made its home. **Osmanthorpe Farm** is derived from 'the *thorp* (outlying farm) of Osmund', this personal name being the Saxon form of the Scandinavian name Asmundr.

Today we expect a road name to be some reference to where it leads to and/or from. An example as such is found in **Allesford Lane**, which led to 'Aelle's ford'.

The gate of St Giles'
church at Edingley.

However, historically names of minor roads described the region alongside the lane. **Greaves Lane** is derived from the Saxon *graefe* meaning 'bush, thicket' and hence this name should be read as being 'the lane running alongside the thicket'.

Edwalton

Domesday lists this place as *Edvvoltone* while almost a century later the record is as *Aedwaldton*. There can be no doubt this name comes from an Old English personal name with *tun* and is 'Eadweald's farmstead'.

It is not often we find pub names which are taken from such a specific point in a region. However, this is where the name of the **Meadow Covert** originates; it was the name of the field on older maps. The sign shows two men attempting to bring down a pheasant flying overhead, yet this is merely artist's interpretation.

Edwinstowe

Domesday's *Edenestou*, *Edenestowa* in 1169, and *Edenestowe* in 1212 all point to a Saxon personal name with Old English *stowe*. This is 'the holy place of St Eadwine', the chapel dedicated to this saint is known to have been here by 1205.

There are a number of local names of interest, including **Bilhaugh** or 'Billa's enclosure'. There is also **Birklands** from Old Scandinavian *lundr* and telling of '(place at) the birch wood', and **Bullifant's Plantation** named from the family of Edwin Bullifant who were here in 1689. Not only people are recorded but also parts of the daily life, the author's favourite kind.

Edwinstowe proclaims itself the village where Robin Hood married his beloved Marion.

Cockglade was once the regular haunt of one species of bird, for it was trapped in sufficient quantities to provide a regular and reliable source of food to be known as 'glade where woodcock are taken'. Another 'hunt' name is found with **King's Stand Farm**, where the king and/or his courtiers would have stood to shoot game. This also tells us something of the quarry, for they would have been raised here solely to give archers the chance to shoot them, hence limiting the kind of creatures which would be found here.

The Sarts is an unusual name, it coming from the Anglo-French *essart* meaning 'woodland clearing'. The meaning is common enough but to find this language as the basis for a place name, even a minor name, is quite rare indeed. **Lidgett House** comes from the more common Old English *hlidgeat* meaning 'swing gate' and a term most commonly found in woodland areas. Lastly there is **Amen Corner**, not named from a 1960s pop group but a region of the parish where the clergy led an annual procession in the ceremony known as 'beating the bounds'. It is thought that this was a remnant of a pre-Christian rite and continued in the hope that it would bless the land for the coming growing season. It has been revived in several places throughout the land.

The local is the **Black Swan**, the origin of which depends upon when the name was first used. If it comes from the eighteenth century or before, it is heraldic, used to signify a very rare or special deed or person. After the discovery of Australia and its resident population of previously unknown black swans, it became a symbolic reference to that faraway land. The obvious clue as to when the pub was built is not as clear cut as one would imagine; there are many examples of pub names being brought by a new landlord so this possibility cannot be discounted.

Egmanton

Even in the twenty-first century this is a very Saxon-sounding name, indeed this is the origin with a personal name suffixed by Old English *tun*. The meaning here is 'Ecgmund's farmstead', although this may not be apparent from the records of *Agemuntone* and *Eggemonton* in 1086 and 1191 respectively.

Two local thoroughfares come from the Old Scandinavian tongue: **Holme Lane** features the element *holmr* meaning 'marsh meadow', while **Hagg Lane** is from *hogg* or 'cutting in woodland', a pathway cleared to provide a shortcut to and from an oft-used destination.

Elkesley

Early records from the eleventh century as *Elchesleie* and in the thirteenth century as *Elkesle*, show the origins to be a Saxon personal name and *leah*. This is 'Ealac's place at the woodland clearing'.

Locally we find minor place names such as **Apleyhead Farm**, not surprisingly 'apple tree clearing' with the addition of 'head' referring to the hill here. **Normanton** is a quite common name, particularly through the north and east of England, where it refers to 'the farmstead of the Norsemen'. It has been stated elsewhere in this book that it is the neighbours who name places; residents simply refer to it as 'home'. Normanton shows this to be the case, for it has the suffix *tun* from Saxon or Old English and names the 'Norsemen', while the residents would have used *by*. There is also **Twyford Bridge**, a later bridge crossing the same stretch as the earlier ford. Indeed, we perhaps should refer to the former river crossing in the plural for the name means 'the double ford (literally two fords)'. It should not be thought this referred to two parallel river crossings, for this is where the rivers Maun and Poulter combine and there is one ford across each just upstream of that point, whereafter it is known as the Idle.

Elston

With early records as *Elvestune* in 1086, *Eluestun* in 1166, *Ayleston* in 1236, and *Eyleston* in 1252 all being markedly different, the first element is somewhat difficult to define with any certainty. Undoubtedly the suffix is Old English *tun* and just as assuredly the first element is a personal name, however here there are several possible offerings. Most likely the name is Scandinavian, perhaps something akin to 'Eilafr's farmstead'. Another name of Norse beginnings is a small road running through Elston. **Lineham Lane** seems to be anything but Scandinavian, although, if English, it is undoubtedly an odd combination of two quite common single-syllable words. The name comes from *lin* and *holmr*, or 'the flax clearing'. Note that the lane likely ran alongside the field of this name and was not the route to or from it.

Elton

A name found several times throughout England, with a number of alternative origins. Here the name was recorded as *Ailetone* in 1086, *Eleton* in 1242, with the modern form sandwiched between the two in 1197. Undoubtedly this is Old English *tun* with a personal name, most likely 'Ella's farmstead' but could also be a pet form of a longer name.

Epperstone

The first element here is a personal name, with the suffix Old English *tun*. With records as *Eprestone* in 1086, *Eperstona* in 1170, and *Eperston* in 1242, the Saxon name is clearly an unusual one. This has been defined as 'Eorphere's farmstead'.

The river here is the site of **Wash Bridge**, a name which would have been unlikely to have existed today if the Saxon inhabitants had not misunderstood that Old Scandinavian *vath* was the equivalent of the Old English *ford*.

It often comes as a surprise to find so many pub names have religious, particularly Christian, connections. Such establishments were normally the only two public buildings in the village and as meeting places were inextricably linked. **Cross Keys** is a name derived from a reference to St Peter, also appearing in the coat of arms of the pope. Note the dedication of the church is the Holy Cross, so the reference to the saint is likely through lands held by the bishopric of Peterborough.

Erewash

A river which forms part of the boundary between the county and neighbouring Derbyshire. One of the major tributaries of the Trent, with its eastern feeder streams it drains much of that corner of the county.

Records of the name are found as *Irewys* in 1145, *Yrewis* in 1175, and *Erwys* in 1601. There is some disagreement as to whether this is Old English *wisce* 'wet meadow' or *irre* 'wandering', or even a combination of the two. Whichever is the true meaning, the inference is exactly the same, the river flooded regularly. That it burst its banks every winter was a boon to the resident farmers, for this brought essential replenishing nutrients to the land.

Obviously a river as substantial as the Erewash must have had a profound effect on those who lived near it. As there had been settlements on or near its banks for many centuries before the arrival of the Saxons, the present name of Saxon origins is clearly not the original. Indeed, the late forms given probably indicate the earlier Celtic name was in use up to the Norman Conquest. However, whatever the previous name was is unknown and will likely remain so.

Everton

Early listings of this name include *Euretone* and *Euerton* in 1086 and 1185 respectively. This shows it comes from Old English *eofor* + *tun*, giving 'the farmstead near where wild boar are seen'.

Harwell is an interesting local name, thought to have come from Old English *here* and *wella* or 'the army springs'. This place is close to the former Roman road which runs from Littleborough in Nottinghamshire to Doncaster in South Yorkshire. It is clear that an army which marched everywhere would have required a clean and reliable water supply and this would have been marked on the map – much as service stations are in the twenty-first century.

F

Fairham Brook

It is very unusual to be able to specify almost exactly when a name came about, but this is one example. This small watercourse joins the Trent at Wilford, but the name comes from south-east of here.

The Ordinance Survey map of 1825 is the first record of this as Fairham Brook. In order to find this name we have to backtrack upstream to Ruddington and Fairham Bridge – a name which is discussed under that listing. In 1346 the upper part of the stream is referred to as *Keuworthbroke*, named after Keyworth which also stands on the waterway.

Farndon

With records such as *Farendone* in 1086, *Ferendon* in 1175, and *Farendon* in 1220, we can see this is an Old English name. Here *fearn + dun* combine to tell us this was 'the hill where ferns grow'; indeed this was probably the name of the place prior to any permanent habitation.

Honey's Lane was used to get to **Honey's Farm**, from which it was named for it was on 'muddy (or sticky) land'.

Farnsfield

The similarity of the first element to that of the previous name is not surprising, both are from the same Old English term. With a record dating from 958 as *Fearnesfeld*, in 1086 as *Farnesfeld*, and in 1187 as *Farnefeld* we can see the suffix in this case is Old English *feld*. This gives a meaning of 'open land where ferns grow'. Once again it is likely that this place was known as such prior to being settled by the Saxons.

A landowner is remembered in a lane at Farnsfield.

Baulker Farm speaks of 'the enclosure marked out by baulks'. Baulks, or timbers, would have reinforced the natural boundaries – although there is the possibility that this place provided some, either as a raw material or where it was stored in a purpose-built building. The idea that Farnsfield may have been a distribution centre for lumber or even timber products may be strengthened by another place name here. **Hexgreave Park** comes from two Old English words, *hekkes* and *graefe* 'the wooden frameworkings in or from the thicket'. Both have never been particularly large places and this may well be further proof that the longevity of the name shows the place was a provider.

Lurcher Farm is derived from the Saxon for 'Leofric's enclosure', while **Combs Farm** and **Combs Wood** tells us this was 'broken land' and used in the sense of 'uneven, not uniform', thus being difficult to work. **Brickyard Lane** was renamed to recall that it gave access to the brickyard. **Quaker Lane** was used by those following this religious group to reach their meeting place. **The Ridgeway** is a new development on an ancient and obvious place name, and the local inn, **The White Post**, had such a simple and yet effective sign.

One of Farnsfield's most famous residents gave his name to **Gregory Gardens**, a small residential side road. Augustus Gregory was born in Farnsfield in August 1819. By the age of ten he found himself in the Swan River Colony in Western Australia, just four months after it had been first settled. In August 1846 he set off on the first of four expeditions over the next twelve years which totalled almost 10,000 miles. The next year he was appointed the surveyor-general of Queensland, a position he held for twenty years until his retirement. A recipient of a knighthood and the Royal Geographical Society's gold medal, he published the journal of his explorations in 1884. He died a bachelor in 1905, having seen more of Australia on horseback than anyone else before or since.

Felley

With listings such as *Feleya* in 1194, *Falleg* in 1240, *Fillay* in 1368, and as the modern form in 1500, this comes from the Old English *fealh* and *leah* describing 'the woodland clearing with fallow land'. From such a description we can deduce something about the history of the place. Fallow land, by design, must have previously been used for growing crops and therefore was settled land before it took this name. This may have been an outlying region of a nearby place, used solely for agricultural purposes before it was settled permanently. Alternatively it was a name applied to a part of a settlement, later to become the name of the place as the previous name fell out of use.

Locally there is **Shipton Hill**, from the Saxon *ceap* + *tun* + *hyll*, which tells us of the 'market settlement by the hill'. Note that the name of the hill has been taken from a place. We also find a name showing us a snapshot of life during the Saxon era in **Cockshutts**, a fairly common name always used to describe 'a corner of land into which woodcock were driven'. The bird being caught and roasted is still considered a delicacy today.

Finningley

Listed as *Feniglei* in 1086, *Feningelay* in 1175, and *Fenyngley* in 1428, this comes from the Saxon or Old English for 'woodland clearing of the fenn dwellers'. Although today it is considered part of South Yorkshire, it has always been a part of Nottinghamshire and, for those residents who still do not consider themselves Yorkshiremen, the name is included in the book of Nottinghamshire.

That this region has long been wetland is reflected, not only in the main name, but also in the local names. **Moize Plantation** comes from the Old English *meos* meaning 'moss' or sometimes used as 'mossy bog'. **Wroot Croft** takes its name from the parish in neighbouring Lincolnshire and can be used to mean 'marshy land' or the 'island in marshy land' where the settlement would have been.

Fiskerton

Another of those names which give an insight into life in the village during Saxon times, so wrongly often referred to as the Dark Ages. From 958 comes the record as *Fircertune*, while Domesday's *Fiscartune* is also fairly accurate. This name is from Old English *fiscere* + *tun* or 'the farmstead of the fishermen'. Standing on the Trent, their catch would have served them four-fold: as food, as a valuable trading commodity, as a feed for their livestock, and the remains would have made an excellent fertiliser for their crops.

Local names show examples of names which have changed little from the original Saxon and others which would be unrecognisable were it not for old records. The former is **Morton**, a name which is virtually unchanged from the original *mor tun* meaning 'the farmstead of or near the moorland'. However, we would be hard pushed to see the latter example as describing 'the valley of the willows', had we nothing earlier than the modern form of **Welladay Bridge**.

Flawborough

Old English is just one of a number of tongues from a group of languages which stretch back to a time of unrecorded history – i.e. before writing. This family is known as the Indo-European Group, itself split into sub-groups including the Germanic, which includes the Scandinavian, Danish, German, Dutch and ultimately English. Sometimes Old English words are uncertain, however there are often very similar words in related languages which can help us in defining a name. Flawborough is but one example. Records of this name are found in Domesday as *Flodberge*, in 1251 as *Flouberewe*, and in 1316 as *Flaubergh*. If we only had Domesday's form, the origin would undoubtedly first be thought to be 'flood', although this does not fit with the topography of the place. Thus we need to find alternatives.

There is an Old English word *floh* which is related to Old Norse *flo* 'layer, stratum' and more importantly Old High German *fluoh* 'rock'. Here we can deduce that *floh* was used to mean 'fragment, bit of stone' and, together with *beorg*, giving us '(place at) the hill with many stones'.

Fledborough

Early listings of this name include *Flatburch* in 1060, *Fladburh* in 1075, *Fladeburg* in 1086, *Flaburc* in 1176, *Fletburg* in 1242, and *Fleburg* in 1275. There can be no doubt this comes from the Saxon describing 'Flaede's fortified place'.

Minor names of note in this area include **Goodhouses Farm** or 'the good enclosures' and featuring the element *(ge)heag*. There is also **Gibraltar** which would normally be seen to be what is known as a remoteness name, an attempt at a humorous reference to the furthest corner of the parish. However, this does not seem to be the reason here for the place is hardly 'remote' in any sense. A look at a map will show this region bears a resemblance to the shape of the isthmus and rock of its more famous namesake standing at the entrance to the Mediterranean, albeit much smaller and topographically dissimilar.

Flintham

As discussed in the introduction, Domesday's records of place names are to be viewed as uncertain. Yet the great census records this place in exactly the same form as that found on twenty-first century road signs. This does not mean that the present form has to be wrong, it could simply be that Domesday has got it right. Indeed, as the only other record of note we have is from 1185 and once again is exactly the same, we must assume that the form is perfectly correct.

The suffix is quite clearly Old English *ham* or 'homestead'. It is a temptation to think the first element refers to the raw material used to produce some of man's earliest tools. However, this sedimentary rock is not found anywhere near here. The real origin is a personal name, giving a definition of 'Flinta's homestead'.

Here is the **Beck Dyke**. Recorded as simply *le Bek* in 1349, the name comes from Old Scandinavian *bekkr* which has the simplistic meaning of 'stream'. This is by no means unusual. Even today we rarely refer to the local river by name but simply as 'the river'. **Inholms Road** is from Old Scandinavian *innam* literally 'piece of land taken in' and meaning 'absorbed, grown into'.

Fosse Way

A road which runs from Exeter to Lincoln and one of the country's most famous Roman roads. If we knew what the name meant, we would be aware it was built by those who occupied these lands for almost four centuries. Records such as *viam de Fosse* in 1250 and *superchiminam Fosse* in 1132 point to the Latin *fossa* meaning simply 'ditch'. Until the Romans arrived there were no ditches alongside roads in England. It is unique in retaining its original Latin name; all other Roman roads are known by Saxon or Old English names.

Fouleville Brook

A name which, certainly correctly, describes it as muddy and overgrown. There is no shortage of records of this name, nor are these lacking any depth. From 1450 comes *Syke called the old Idle*, in 1650 this was *Foule evill*, and by 1825 *Foul Evil Brook*. There is no doubt that this is meant to describe 'the muddy or fouled brook'. It seems the record from the fifteenth century deemed this to be an old free-flowing watercourse; this may or may not be the case.

Fulwood

The earliest known listing of this name is as *Folewode* in the thirteenth century. Both of these Old English elements are found quite often in place names. Here *ful* + *wudu* combine to give the '(place at) the foul wood'.

The element 'foul' is more normally used to describe a water source, i.e. stagnant, dirty, muddy, unusable – particularly for livestock. It is uncertain as to the meaning of such a name. Whether it is suggesting woodland with a dirty pond, an overgrown and badly rotted woodland area, or perhaps a dumping ground or midden, will doubtless remain unknown. However, it does bode the question, if the area was noticeably *ful*, why settle here?

G

Gamston

There are only two places of any size with this name in the whole of England, both of these are in Nottinghamshire, both earliest records are in Domesday and are identical (as *Gamelestune*), and both have exactly the same origin. However, this is pure coincidence and they are otherwise completely unconnected. This name is derived from a Scandinavian personal name with Old English *tun*, giving 'Gamall's farmstead'.

Here we find **Muttonhill Bridge**, this being taken from a nickname for 'the hill with good pasture for sheep'.

The inn at Gamston is the **Goose**, named after the famous goose fair held in Nottingham. Lasting for three days each October it dates from the thirteenth century when it soon became the largest event of its kind in Europe. It takes something major to prevent the annual spectacle going ahead; so far it has missed 1646 due to the bubonic plague and the years of both world wars in the twentieth century.

Gedling

Although there are three records of this name, none of them really show the exact nature of the personal name which precedes Old English *ingas*. In 1086 it was as *Ghellinge*, in 1187 *Gedlinges*, and in 1249 *Gedelinghes*, all of which tell us this was the '(settlement of) the family or followers of Gedel or Gedla'.

In a document dating from 1792 we find a record of *the Beck*. Described then as a 'rivulet', today it is known as the **Ouse Dyke** which is crossed via **Ouse Bridge**. This basic name is an ancient one indeed, seen several times throughout our islands. Celtic in origin, the name means simply 'water'.

Minor names in the parish include **Podder Farm**. From Middle English *pode* this describes 'the frog enclosure'. Despite the grammar this does not suggest frogs were being farmed, simply they were here, and in significant numbers too. This also informs us the area must once have been decidedly wet for much of the year, for amphibian skin will not tolerate drying out. The frogs are not the only former residents to have left their mark on the names around Gedling. A document of 1850 reveals the names of William Jessop and Abraham Musson, still seen on today's maps as **Jessop's Lane** and **Musson's Lane** respectively.

Gilt Brook

While this name is found to the north-west of Nottingham, the brook takes its name from much further north than that. At Kirkby in Ashfield stands **Gilt Bridge**, itself coming from where it stands on 'the kilted piece of land' – i.e. a strip of land bordering one side of this brook. Hence a small area of arable land gave its name to the bridge which was then applied to the brook. This clearly happened because those who gave the name to the brook had no idea why the name was applied to the bridge.

Girton

Here is a name listed in Domesday as *Gretone*. This name, found more than once in England, always comes from Old English *geot* + *tun* 'the farmstead on gravelly ground'.

Also here, is an old water-filled stretch of the Trent called **The Fleet**. A document of 1348 describes the *fishery called le Flete*, and from around the same time *auam que dicitur Holde trent* which means exactly the same as the 1607 listing of *a ditch called Old Trent*. This is from the Old English *fleot* meaning 'a stretch of water' – a far better description than that of the seventeenth century as a 'ditch'.

More than one generation of schoolboys have derived hours of amusement from the local name of **Weecar**. The origin here is Old Scandinavian *kiarr* meaning 'marsh' with a Middle English *wee* or 'small'.

Gonalston

Whether read as Domesday's *Gunnuluestone* or the late twelfth-century *Gunnoluiston*, this name is seen as a Scandinavian and Saxon hybrid. Here the Old English *tun* follows a name which is known from coinage – not that the individual on the artefact should be considered in any way related to the founder of the settlement. Gonalston began life as 'Gunnulf's farmstead'.

Spital is a fairly common minor place name, although it might not be instantly recognised as an abbreviated form of 'hospital'. This hospital reminds us of the early building specifically for tending to the sick founded by William de Heriz. Prior to this the place was named **Broadbusk**, which shows the area was influenced by both Saxon and Scandinavian settlers during its time. A combination of Old English *brad* and Old Scandinavian *buskr* gives '(the place at) the broad bush'.

Gotham

Nothing irritates the locals more than having this place pronounced in the manner of the fictitious city in which comic-book superhero Batman is the scourge of a series of increasingly odd villains. The correct pronunciation of the first element here is exactly as the Saxons intended *gat* + *ham* 'goat homestead'. In 1085 the name is found as Gatham (the perfect Old English form), in 1152 it was listed as *Gataham*, while by 1291 the modern form is first seen.

One local pub is named the **Cuckoo Bush**. This does not refer to the bird with little parenting skills and a call recognised by all. This is named after one of the narratives from the well-known *Wise Men of Gotham*. These tales centre around men whose actions are anything but wise; indeed the title is clearly as ironic as the tales themselves. There is no suggestion that the twenty or so stories, which first appeared in print in 1540, refer to exclusively to men of Gotham. In fact the only reason the village is cited in the title seems to be because the man who collected these stories and put them in print, Andrew Borde, was somehow associated with the place. Why he chose Gotham is uncertain for he was born in Sussex. There is a Gotham in Sussex but it is only a minor district in the village of Hailsham. It has been suggested that Henry VIII commissioned the publication in order to raise money to deal with a major poaching problem in Gotham, yet this is recorded many years afterwards and seems to have been created to answer the question.

There were many more stories of the actions of fools collected than the published twenty. The tale of the cuckoo is the third in the book but has always been the best known. It speaks of the men of the village hearing the sound of the cuckoo calling from the bush. The sound of the cuckoo calling to attract potential mates is one of the most easily recognised signs of spring. In order to preserve the delights of spring for eternity the men devised a plan to keep the bird in the bush. Thus the men set about building a hedge and fence around the bush to ensure the bird stayed there and continued to voice the call which gives it its name. Eventually the bird flies away and the men voice the punchline when they realise, 'If only we had made the hedge higher she would never have escaped.' The bush is said to have been located on a hill above the village where, today, the remains of an ancient mound can be found.

The Sun Inn is a fairly common pub name and comes from that list of welcoming pub names. The return of the sun, be it in the morning or after a long winter, is enough to make everyone feel better. This idea transferred itself readily to a pub name, while producing a simple and relatively inexpensive sign.

The Cuckoo Bush public house. Built in 1858, it is a reminder of the Wise Men of Gotham.

Granby

For those who already know something of place name origins, the name of Granby would seem to be wholly from the Old Scandinavian language. A quick examination of records such as *Granebi, Grenebi, Granebi* and *Graneby* (1086 to 1252) serves only to confirm this. This name comes from 'Grani's farmstead', with the element *by* being the Scandinavian equivalent of Saxon *tun* and which is just as common.

A stream here is known as **Rundle Beck**, the term coming from the Old French *rondelle* or Middle English *rondel* with Old Scandinavian *bekkr* telling us this is 'the round stream'. Indeed its course does appear very circular. In 1240 this is recorded as *Plungarebeck*, named after Plungar in neighbouring Leicestershire.

Grassthorpe

As with the previous name of Granby this is another example of the Scandinavian influence in the county prior to the Norman Conquest. Here the two elements of *gres* + *thorp* combine to give an origin of 'the grass farmstead'. This is rather an unusual, indeed possibly even a unique name. Clearly the idea is to communicate the idea that the pasture here was of quite excellent quality, however this would usually be alluded to by some other means – 'dairy farm', 'butter producer', 'where calves are reared', or the like. It seems likely that this place had excellent pasture which was used for a variety of reasons over a reasonably short period of time otherwise the use would be stated in the name and not simply the grass.

Greasley

The early forms of *Griseleia* in 1086, *Greseley* in 1230, and *Greselly* in 1272, all point to a probable Old English *greosn* + *leah*. While the first element here is by no means certain, we can only assume this is '(place at) the gravelly woodland clearing' in the absence of any other evidence.

Local names include **Beauvale**, which was listed in 1331 as *domus de Bello Valle*. This comes from the French for 'the beautiful valley' and is easily seen as being related to Belvoir in neighbouring Leicestershire, albeit with a markedly different pronunciation. The rather unusual name of **Big Stainers**, first seen in 1550, simply refers to 'the pasture clearing'.

Another odd name is that of **Brookbreasting Farm**, with the main name having become corrupted from the original 'brook bursting' and a suggestion that the Gilt Brook has a tendency to flood.

Brookhill Leys has evolved from the Old English *broc*, which can be understood as referring to a badger, and the name 'pasture by the badger holes'. **Lynn Croft** was named from a field which was originally 'the flax field or enclosure', flax once being a much more valuable commodity than it is today.

The name of **Newthorpe** comes from Old English speaking of 'the new outlying farm', a seasonal farmstead which soon grew to become a permanent community.

Watnall refers to one of the original settlers in this community, describing '(the place at) Watta's spur of land'. Later on, in 1633, a William Watsone was resident in Greasley who gave his name to **Watson's Wood**, while 'the clearing bordered by willow trees' gave rise to **Willeywood Farm**, **Willey Spring** and **Willey Lane**.

Gringley on the Hill

None of the early records shows the addition which requires no explanation. These early forms are found as *Gringeleia* in 1086, *Gringelay* in 1184, *Gringeleg* in 1234, *Gringele* in 1252, and *Gryngeleia* in 1316. Here the Old English origin is most likely *grene* + *inga* + *leah* 'the green woodland clearing of the people'. However, it is possible that the first element is a reference to a similarly named place just

6 miles away, known as Little Gringley. In order for this alternative to be viable, Little Gringley would have to have been founded first and people from there needed to have moved to resettle at its namesake on the hill. In this case the meaning would be 'the woodland clearing of the people of Gringley'. The place is near East Retford.

A couple of local names speak not of the locality, but of those who held the lands. Over the years, portions have been held by the Duke of Portland, as evidenced by **Duke's Drain**, and the Duchy of Lancaster, remembered by **Lancaster Road**.

Grove

Recorded as *Graue* in 1086 and *Graua* in 1194, this is a common minor place name from Old English *graf* simply meaning '(place at) the grove or copse'. In fact, from the point of view of place names, the only remarkable thing about Grove is that it has not attracted a second distinguishing element.

The same cannot be said about a field name here, **Clapgate**. This can be defined as 'swing gate', a common enough feature in many fields today but not when the name was first coined. Any name would be given in order to make it recognisable and, whenever possible, make it unique within the region. Knowing this we can be certain that this was where the first such gate was seen within the area. Furthermore, such a simple idea would have spread quite quickly so maybe this was the original in the county, or even the country.

Gunthorpe

A name found in several places, and normally with the first element being a personal name of Gunni. However, Nottinghamshire's Gunthorpe is different. Early forms of *Gunnetorp* in 1086, *Gunildethorp* in 1191, and *Gunnetorp* in 1193 show this refers to a female name and is 'Gunnhildr's outlying farmstead' with the second element from Old Scandinavian *thorp*.

The local river here is the **Dover Beck**; as with the Devon River this has absolutely no connection with its namesake and has totally different origins. This is an ancient name, a name which has been corrupted so much it is a little difficult to know which language it comes from although the meaning is identical. We are certain it is a Celtic or British tongue; these ancient origins are always extremely simple. Here it is either Celtic *dubro* or Welsh *dwfr*, both meaning 'water'. In later years the Old Scandinavian *bekkr* was added giving 'water stream'. If this seems overly simplistic, remember even today we rarely mention the local river by name, normally referring to it as just 'the river'.

The **Order Beck** is a tributary which seems to have been named before the rest of the Dover, for it has a name meaning 'the old stream'.

There is an interesting and fairly unusual name here, that of **Marlock House**. It is not the form which is different but the origin, coming from two Old English elements which are not often seen in place names. Here *mearth* 'marten or weasel' with *lacu* 'stream' tells us such creatures were commonplace around here. It is particularly unusual to find two rare elements such as this in combination. However, the meaning is certain.

The Anchor is a well-used pub name and for a number of reasons, not least because it is a very simple and easily recognised shape. At Gunthorpe the sign is clearly a nautical one which probably indicates an early owner or landlord had some connection to the sea. In pub names **The Unicorn** is always heraldic. However, it is such a popular element in so many coats of arms it is virtually impossible to discover the etymology.

H

Habblesthorpe

If we take the forms of *Happelesthorp* in 1154, *Happelestorp* in 1275, and *Harplesthorp* in 1341, it seems certain that this is a personal name together with Old Scandinavian *thorp*. While hybrid names are not unusual, it is strange to find the suffix from Scandinavian with what is apparently a Saxon individual's name. This seems to be 'Haeppel's outlying farmstead', yet it is possible the forms are corrupted and the personal name is Scandinavian of a similar vein.

Halam

The earliest record of this name dates from 958 as *Healum*, the only later listing of note that of *Halum* which is seen consistently from 1198. This is doubtless from the Old English *halh* in a plural form, *halum*, describing a '(place at) the nooks or corners of land'. What is surprising is to find it alone; normally this is only seen as a suffix (usually to a personal name).

This is near the source of the River Greet, although it is not known by that name here. Once, when communication was limited to the speed of the fastest horse and travel was a major undertaking, rivers of any length must have had several names. Indeed, it is quite possible that several rivers were known by one name on one bank and a completely different name on the opposite side. When maps were first produced, the cartographer would have labelled the river with the name which he knew first. Thus today it is rare to find a river with more than one name, yet here is one example for here the young river is still known as **Halam Beck**. The latter part comes from the Old Scandinavian *bekkr* meaning 'stream', while the first part is a case of back-formation from the place name. It seems likely that this is not the original name of the stream, although it was recorded as *Halumbek* in 1330.

Among the names found within the parish are **Goldhill** or 'the hill where marigolds grow'. While this particular flower is cited there is no reason to believe it was not some other similarly coloured flower, it is simply that this is the most commonly found in minor place names. The name of **Brockley** has hardly changed since the original Saxon *broc leah* 'the woodland clearing where badgers are seen'. Clearly this is not a particularly unique name, especially as a minor or district name. One name unique to Halam is **Machin's Farm**, or at least unique to Thomas Machin who was here in 1635.

A Halam road sign.

The local here is **The Waggon and Horses**, the sign depicting the harvest and the hay being pulled along by horse in a traditional scene. The spelling is the correct one, although in recent times normal use has produced the alternative 'wagon'. The sign may show a harvest but the name originates from when the harvest was transported to the inn which then acted as agents to hold the produce until it was collected, for a small fee of course.

Halloughton

Records of *Healhtune* 958 and *Halton* in 1291, together with the modern form seem barely related. However, related they are and from the Old English *halh* + *tun*, giving us the definition of 'farmstead in a nook of land'.

St James' church, Halloughton.

Harby

This name has two possible origins, both from Old Scandinavian. Either this is 'Herrothr's farmstead', or 'farmstead with a herd or flock' – the latter from *hjorth* + *by*. Listed in the eleventh century as *Herdebi* and *Herdrebi* and in the late thirteenth century as *Hertheby*, without other clues it will remain difficult to define this place with any certainty.

There is a very interesting minor place name here, possibly a unique one. From Old English or Saxon *ryding* comes **Wallrudding**, very easily seen to have the meaning of '(the place at) the walled clearing'.

Harworth

This name is found in Domesday as *Hareworde*, with later listings of *Harewrthe* in 1191 and *Harewurth* in 1242. This is an Old English name from *har* + *worth* speaking of 'the enclosure on the boundary'. The place is on a long-standing border with neighbouring Yorkshire.

Within the parish is found **Hesley Hall**, which speaks of 'the hazel clearing, or hazel wood', a name which gives us an instant image of the trees surrounding the glade before the first settlers arrived. There is also **Serlby**, an Old Scandinavian place name meaning 'Serle's village'. However, while **Martin** seems to be another having its origins in a personal name, it is actually a corruption of the original 'boundary farmstead'. **Limpool** is a district name derived from the Old English or Saxon telling us of 'the pool by the lime trees'.

Haughton

This is a common name seen in several places around the north of England, all having the same meaning of 'farmstead on or near the nook of land'. All, that is, except the example found in Nottinghamshire. Listed as *Hoctun* in Domesday, this is not from the usual *halh* + *tun* but Old English *hoh* + *tun* or 'the farmstead on a spur of land'.

Hawksworth

Early forms of this name are quite plentiful. In 1086 it is *Hochesuorde*, in 1179 *Houkeswrda*, in 1188 *Houkeswurda*, and in 1236 *Hokiswrh*. Here is an Old English name with a personal name followed by *worth* giving 'Hoc's enclosure'.

Also here is **Car Dyke**, a name from Old Scandinavian *kiarr sik* 'the marsh ditch', constructed to enable the land to drain for the growing season.

Hawton

Listed as *Holtone* and *Houtone* in the eleventh century, and as *Houton* and *Hautone* in the thirteenth century, this name is derived from two Old English elements *hol* + *tun* or 'the farmstead in a hollow'.

Hayton

Listed as *Heiton* in 1175, this name is found all over England and is always from Old English *heg* + *tun* giving 'the farmstead where hay is stored or produced'.

Joining the River Idle here is **Gun's Beck**, found as *Gunsbeck* in 1762. The end is Old Scandinavian *bekkr* 'stream'. The first element is almost certainly a personal name from the same place, a remnant of the days when they held much of the land in the north and east of England. The forms known are rather late and not very different from the modern record, thus it is difficult to tie it down but is probably something not unlike the man's name Gunni or the woman's name Gunnhildr.

Minor names in this area include **Tiln**. Listings of this as a place are found in Domesday as *Tille*, yet by 1524 there are two distinct settlements known as *Northtill* and *Southtill*. Today there is only one and it is not clear what happened to the other. Possibly the two grew together to form one settlement, or maybe one is now lost beneath the concrete of modern society.

The etymology of the name of Tiln has always been disputed. One suggestion is that it was an alternative name for the river from *tilan ea*, literally 'useful river' and suggesting a source of power. Now the river in question is the Idle and, as seen under its own listing, can hardly be both lazy and a method of powering a watermill, making this definition implausible.

However, if the origin is *tilan eg*, 'serviceable area in marshland', it makes a great deal more sense. Here the reference is not to the river but the settlement, which would have occupied one of the few dry regions in the area.

Another interesting name is that of **Old Ea Drain**, a name which is found as *The Old Ea* in 1762 and *Old Eau* in 1825. This second record here is the most telling, and the latter part of that record may well be recognised by those with even the smallest smattering of French, *eau* being the word for 'water'. The word is found regularly in place names around fenland.

Here is also found **Goit Lane**, which comes from Middle English *gote* and means literally 'watercourse', the inference being, permanent flowing water alongside this lane, although it would have existed well before the lane and would have been the main factor in dictating the course of the path. **Smeeth Lane** is also found here, a name which is probably still recognisable as 'smooth place' from Middle English *smethe*. This would have been a region, possibly arable land, where stones and other imperfections were entirely absent. Overlooking the area is

Hollin Hill, a name from Old English *holegn* speaking of this being 'the hill where holly grows'.

Haywood Oaks

The early thirteenth century sees two records of this name, as *Heywood* and *Heywud*. This is from the Old English *haeg* + *wudu* '(place at) the enclosed wood'. The addition must be a comparatively recent addition, no doubt referring to some oaks of note either because of their size or their location.

Headon

Domesday's record of *Hedune* probably shows the origin here is Old English *heah* + *dun*, telling us this settlement was at the 'high hill'.

Hickling

A place name which, at first glance, sounds very Scandinavian. However the records of *Hilkelinge* in about 1000, *Hichelinge* in 1086, and *Hikelinga* in 1185 show this is another of Saxon derivation, telling of '(the settlement) of the family or followers of Hicel'. Here the personal name is followed by *inga*, an element normally found as the middle of three and followed by '-ham' or '-ton', something which has clearly not been the case with Hickling. This name being derived from the people, and not from the place, may be an indication that this settlement was a result of a relocation.

Very close to Hickling runs the **Dalby Brook**, a tiny tributary of the Smite. In 1533 this is recorded as *a ryndill called Dalbie broke*. The Old English *rynel* meant 'small stream' but eventually the whole course took on its Leicestershire name. The name of Dalby means 'village in a valley or dale'.

Hockerton

This name is of Old English origins in *hocer* + *tun* 'the farmstead at or near the hump or rounded hill'. The first element here is not commonly found in place names, but is more often seen to describe a disfigurement of an animal or individual, which is probably suggesting the supposed 'hill' was less than a few feet high. Early records of this name are found from the eleventh to the thirteenth centuries as *Hocretune*, *Hochertun*, *Hocretona* and *Hokerinton*.

As with Hawksworth, there is a **Car Dyke** of identical origins, 'the marsh ditch'. **Whitestubb Lane** is recorded as *le white stubb* during the fifteenth century. This refers to a lump of land alongside this lane which is quite obviously white. A document from 1707 refers to **Birds Farm** as being the home of Thomas Bird at this time and almost certainly home to his family for some time before this.

Hodsock

Over the centuries this name has been listed as *Odesach* in 1086, *Hoddishac* in 1204, *Hoddeshok* in 1232, *Hoddeshak* in 1242, and *Hodeshok* in 1250. There can be no doubt this has originated from the Saxon or Old English for 'Hodd's oak', although the propensity for dropping the initial 'h' today may make the future evolution and definition of the name interesting!

Locally we find a wealth of interesting names, including **Fleecethorpe Farm** which comes from 'Flick's outlying farmstead' – and while the individual is unknown, we do know this is a very specifically Danish name. A Saxon gentleman who gave his name to a place was Heremod whose *tun* is today known as **Hermeston Hall**.

There are a number of places named after people, including **Winks Wood**. In truth there is no record of anyone of that name in Hodsock, although in 1840 there was a Joseph Winks in neighbouring Carlton and it is safe to assume a relative provided the name here. **Bumblebee Hall** sounds as if it would have an interesting and complex etymology. However, in reality it is simply a nickname.

There is also the name of **Toad's Hole Wood**, which is often defined as 'toad holes' and suggesting this is marshy ground. In truth the region could be said to be a reasonable amphibian habitat, yet this has nothing to with the origins of the name. This is 'the wood where fox holes are found', this is nothing to do with warfare but refers to the animal – traditionally the fox has always been referred to as tod.

Holbeck

Only two early listings for this name are found, as *Holebek* in 1180 and as *Holbek* in 1332. These forms are certainly Old Scandinavian but leave the second element unclear. This name may be either *holr* + *bekkr* '(settlement at) the stream in the hollow' or *hol* + *bekkr* '(settlement at) the hollow stream' – the second alternative of 'hollow stream' referring to one which disappears underground.

Here we also find other names of Old Scandinavian origin such as **Collingthwaite** meaning 'Colling's clearing or paddock'. There is also the rather strange **Bonbusk**, which has changed but little since the original *bondi buskr* or 'scrubland occupied by a *bondi* or peasant farmer'. Finally there is a field known as **The Old Hag**. Not what we might think (although that will have affected it somewhat), this comes from *hogg*, speaking of 'a path cut through woodland'.

Holme

A common place name, often found in combination with a second distinguishing element. Here the origins are Old Scandinavian *holmr* which is literally 'island' but more often refers to dryer ground in land which is marshland if even only seasonally. The earliest record of this name is exactly as in the modern form dating from 1203.

Holme Pierrepont

Another Holme, some 15 miles north-east of the previous entry and a much earlier settlement. Famous for its National Watersports Centre, it has identical origins to that of the previous entry and is from Old Scandinavian *holmr* 'dry ground in marsh'. A quick look at even modern maps can quickly show how this place may have acquired such a description.

While Domesday records this place as simply *Holmo*, the earliest record of the addition is from 1571 as *Holme Peyrpointe*. This sixteenth-century record is significant because it shows a fair approximation of the modern pronunciation, while the modern spelling is much closer to the original. Furthermore, the very late record of this manorial name is also of interest, for it shows the family's influence over the centuries. Indeed it is documented that Annora de Perpunt held this manor in 1303, later acquired by her husband Sir Henry Pierpont. The family name comes from a French place name of Pierrepont, of which there are several, and all of which refer to '(the place at) Pierre's bridge'.

The local name of **Adbolton** has been influenced by modern names, although pronunciation has also influenced the evolution. In Domesday it is *Alboltune* and in 1242 *Alwalton*. Yet taking the local pronunciation and records into consideration, the personal name is undoubtedly closer to a name resembling 'Eadbeald's farmstead'. Similarly, the region of **Bassingfield** also features a Saxon personal name and comes from 'the open country of the people or followers of Bassa'.

Hoveringham

Listed as *Horingeham* in 1086, *Houeringeham* in 1167, and in the modern form as early as 1235 – a surprising find considering the age and the number of characters in the name. This seems to come from the Old English *hofer* + *inga* + *ham*, which would give 'the homestead of the people who live at the hump-shaped hill'. However, the element *inga* is normally found following a personal name and, if this is the case, may well indicate a nickname such as Hofera. It is certain that if such a nickname did exist it would not have been a complimentary one, probably describing someone with a noticeable deformity.

The names of **Lansic House** and **Lansic Lane** have two possible origins. While it is difficult to decide which is the most likely beginning from the records, logically *lang sic* or 'the long drainage ditch' is the favourite. There are suggestions the name could be from *land sic* or 'the land drainage ditch' which, while it fits the written forms, does not particularly stand out – all drainage ditches were natural or man-made features to drain the land – thus there is little support for this alternative.

Regulars at the **Reindeer Inn** might have pondered the origins of the name of their local, however, the creature's association with Christmas can be the only reason for its choice. There seems to be no heraldic link, or a family name. It should be noted that there are a surprising number of pubs of this name and even more modern minor streets named in honour of St Nicholas's preferred mode of power. As the name does not appear anywhere near as popular in other counties, it may have some other significance which has yet to be discovered.

Hucknall

Records of this name date from Domesday as *Hochenale, Huccenhal* in 1163, *Hukenhal* in 1198 and *Huckenhale* also in 1198. As with its namesake in nearby Derbyshire, this name comes from an Old English personal name with *hlaw*. This tells us it was 'Hucca's nook of land'. Historically there is a reference here to **Hucknall Torkard**, the addition to differentiate between this and the place in Derbyshire. The addition, we know, refers to the Norman family who held this manor, namely Geoffrey Torchard in 1195 and John Torcard in 1235.

Here flows the **Nunn Brook**. Recorded as *Nunne Brooke poole* in 1650, it clearly ran near or through a region associated with a convent or the sisters.

Other local names include **Farleys** from *fearn leah* 'the woodland clearing where bracken grows'. **The Nabbs** comes from Old Scandinavian *nabbi* referring to the hill and describing it as literally 'pointed' and used to mean 'a peak'. **Butler's Hill** recalls former resident Henry Butler who was here in 1654, while **Leiver's Hill** is named after a family who have been here for centuries and who are still here today.

The name of **Misk** is an unusual place name. It comes from a well known Saxon word *mix*. Despite how this word is used today, it was originally used to describe 'dung'. It may seem to be another example of a name applied to unproductive land, however it may simply be where such was collected and later used as a fertiliser.

Local street names include **Coates Avenue** named after composer Eric Coates, who penned 'By The Sleepy Lagoon' – better known as the signature tune to the

BBC radio programme *Desert Island Discs*, and who was born in Hucknall in August 1886. **Byron Street** is, somewhat predictably, named after the poet and philosopher Lord Byron who was buried in the parish church on 16 July 1824. **Lovelace Walk** is named after Ada Lovelace, daughter of Lord Byron who is also buried in the church, and who is considered as the first computer programmer having aided in the studies of Babbage's famous machine. **Blatherwick Close** remembers Steve Blatherwick, who played football for Nottingham Forest, Wycombe Wanderers, Hereford United, Reading, Burnley and Chesterfield and who was a son of the town. **Beardsmore Grove** is named after John Henry Beardsmore, who wrote the history of the town first published in 1909.

A number of pubs around Hucknall are worthy of examination, for they represent every age of the pub name and most of the areas from which they are taken. One of the earliest known pub signs, and therefore names, is **The Chequers**. Originally it referred to the board being hung outside to show that, besides fine wines, good food and pleasant company, a board game could be played to pass the time. Innkeepers were also seen in later times as money lenders, where the sign then gave us the word 'exchequer', still the financial head of the nation. The **Nabb Inn** features a name which is used in a number of English pubs and in place names, and which may be easier to recognise as being at the summit of the hill. **The Portland Arms** is another name found around the country, always referring to the Dukes of Portland. These great landowners are descended from Hans Bentinck, favourite of William III. 'Stars' are popular for pub names, originally because of the religious connection and that they were a simple sign to produce and to recognise. Indeed, this may well have been the reason it was chosen as part of the coat of arms of the Worshipful Company of Innkeepers. With so many 'Stars' around it was inevitable there would be a second distinguishing addition as in the **Seven Stars** here in Hucknall. **The Romans** is not as common a pub name as may be expected considering they took the nation under its wing as part of the great empire. Although they left over fifteen hundred years ago they were here for four centuries and certainly influenced life here considerably.

Hucknall was a testing station for the world's first vertical take-off and landing aircraft. As the first design was only to test the theories and never intended the fly, there was little resemblance to an aircraft. It is not difficult to visualise what it resembled as it was immediately christened **The Flying Bedstead**, and the pub took the name. The craft was eventually developed into an actual model and when it made its debut it was known as **The Harrier**. And so another pub name was born.

Huthwaite

Records of this name are plentiful, found as *Hothweit* in 1208, *Hothweyt* in 1288, *Houthwayt* in 1330, and *Howthwaite* in 1611. This is a hybrid name with an Old English *hoh* combining with Old Scandinavian *thveit* to give '(place at) the clearing on a spur of land'.

Blackwell Brook finds its way west from here to join the Erewash in Derbyshire. The basic name is Saxon or Old English *blaec wielle* meaning 'the dark stream', the additional 'Brook' is comparatively recent and really superfluous.

Herrods Hill has no biblical connections but recalls former resident John Herrod, who was here in 1850. The name of **Rooley Wood** is easy enough to define; the basic name means 'the rough clearing in the wood'. However, today the name has the additional 'wood' and is the name of a field. What is left of the wood today stands alongside the field from which it took its name, the field having taken its name from the clearing within the same wood.

Pub names which mention a coat of arms, or even a part of it, do not always refer to invididuals. Indeed there are many named because of the potential customers in the area. Nottinghamshire being one of the counties associated with mining meant it was inevitable there would be a **Miners Arms**. The sense of camaraderie and welcoming within is not just restricted to one trade but to all at the uniquely named **Workpeoples Inn**.

In and around this part of the country there has been a great deal of influence by the Manners family, the dukes of Rutland. It is likely this is representative of the family, taken from the coat of arms.

I

Idle

One of the county's most prominent rivers is found recorded as *Idlae* in 750, *Iddil* in 958, *Idle* in about 1000, and *Yddel* in 1302. This seems to be from Old English *idel* meaning literally 'idle, lazy'. If this is so it means this river formed by the confluence of the Maun and the Meden is named because of its slow current speed as it meanders across the flood plain.

The names of rivers, especially the larger rivers, are normally much older and from the Celtic languages. Perhaps this name does come from an unknown word and is related to the Breton river name Isole. If so, the meaning would be unchanged, simply the source would need to be different and likely to be from a tongue of the very early Indo-European group.

K

Kelham

This is a very Scandinavian sounding name and it is this ancient tongue which has given rise to this place name. Records such as *Chelum* in about 1155, *Chelun* in 1166, and *Kelum* in the twelfth century show this to be from a plural form of *kjolr* and is the '(place at) the ridges'.

Locally we find **Park Leys** which, very unusually, has a second element which has been misinterpreted. It is easy to see how the Old English *leah* or 'woodland clearing' has become the acccepted form for this name, it is among the most common suffixes in England. However, the real ending here is Old Scandinavian *hlada* with the completely different meaning of 'barn', hence the name can be interpreted as 'the park or estate with a barn'. Furthermore we can infer from this, as place names invariably mark something unusual or very different, that the barn was either a building which stood out from the rest or where something in particular was kept or housed.

Kersall

A number of early forms are found for this place name – *Cherueshale* in 1086, *Kyrneshale* in 1196, *Kyrueshal* in 1197, and *Kirneshall* in 1264. This is likely to be an Old English personal name with a suffix *halh*, thus the origin would be '(place at) the nook of land of a man called Cynehere'.

Keyworth

There are a number of records of this place name, although these are not conclusive and some uncertainty as to the first element remains. As can be seen from listings

A Keyworth road sign.

such as *Caworde* in 1086, *Kaworda* in 1178, *Kewurda* in the twelfth century, *Kieword* in 1201, and *Kewurth* in 1242, there are distinct differences and no element stands out more than the rest. The suffix here is certainly Old English *wic* meaning 'enclosure', which could well be preceded by a personal name.

However, some sources have suggested this may be *caeg* + *worth*, which would give 'the enclosure made from poles'. Now the general use of *worth* is to describe an enclosure which is protection for their livestock during hours of darkness, not a barrier to protect the people. As such the barriers would not have been natural, as with a hedge for a field, but a purpose-built fence or pallisade. It is difficult to imagine such a fence which is not made from poles, thus this alternative seems improbable as it has nothing to distinguish it from any other enclosure.

Doubtless one local name has provided hours of mirth for generations of children. However, the name of **Nicker Hill** is derived from a dialect word for a woodpecker.

The sign in Keyworth town square.

Kilvington

A name found in neighbouring Yorkshire too, each with the same origin. Recorded in the eleventh century as *Chelvinctune* and *Cheluintone*, with a *Kilvintun* in 1236. This is of Old English derivation, a personal name followed by *ing + tun*. Thus Kilvington was originally 'the farmstead of the family or followers of Cylfa or Cynelaf'.

Kimberley

Whether the modern female name was influenced by this place is dubious, however it certainly did not originate from here. This is an Old English name with the suffix *leah*, telling us it was originally '(place at) the woodland clearing of a man called Cynemaer'. Early records of this name have been found in Domesday as *Chinemarelie* and around 1200 as *Kinemarle*.

   The name of **Babbington** has been taken from the place near Coventry. It came along with the new lord of the manor, one Hugo de Babington, who arrived here around the fourteenth century. It seems certain this place existed prior to this and probably had another name, although what that name was is unknown.

Pubs in the area recall a number of individuals, some better known than others. **Queen Adelaide**, after whom the city in Australia was named, was the consort of William IV. Often described as 'England's greatest hero', Horatio Nelson is still honoured by pubs being named after him today. Clearly there is a desire to make each place individual; this would have been one reason why the **Lord Nelson and Railway** appears, although the addition was only from the time when the train network came to Kimberley.

Not all of the figures in history were as well known. **Lord Clyde**, otherwise known as Sir Colin Campbell, was a distinguished soldier who attained the rank of field marshal. Popular with his men, other military leaders considered his safety first approach overly cautious and gave him the rather unkind nicknames such as 'Old Slowcoach' and 'Sir Crawling Camel'. He is best remembered for his Relief of Lucknow in India in 1858. The following year his efforts were rewarded by him being made Baron Clyde of Clydesdale. There is no direct link between this Glasgow-born solider and Nottinghamshire, so either it was named (or possibly renamed) as news of the victory filtered through or maybe an early owner or landlord (or a close family member) was involved in the action.

Kingston on Soar

There are a great number of places with names from 'the farmstead of the king'. However, the Nottinghamshire name is different. This is still of Old English derivation, but from *cyning* + *tun* meaning '(place at) the royal stone'. The addition is at least a Celtic, or possibly earlier, river name meaning 'the flowing one'.

The bridge at Kingston on Soar.

Kinoulton

With records from 971 as *Kinildetune*, in 1086 it was *Chineltune*, by 1152 *Cheneldestona*, and by 1211 *Kinelton*. Here is a Saxon personal name with Old English *tun*, with an origin of 'farmstead of a woman called Cynehild'.

Two local names remember former residents. **Clarke's Bridge** stands on land associated with John Clarke, who was here in 1712, while **Kemp's Spinney** is named after George Kemp, a resident of Kinoulton by 1840.

The local inn is the **Neville Arms**, a reference to the Earls of Warwick who, at their most powerful, were among the largest landowners in the country.

Kirkby in Ashfield

In the region of England largely under Scandinavian influence, Kirkby is a common name. Indeed the origins are Old Scandinavian from *kirkju* + *by* 'the village with a church'.

The number of examples concentrated into a reasonably small area have made an additional distinctive element almost obligatory. Here the name almost tells you the addition is that of an old district name, itself from Old English *aesc* + *feld* 'open land where ash-trees grow'.

Local names here include **The Grives**, which is from Old Norse *gryfja* meaning 'hole or pit', and a reference to the region being in an obvious and well-defined valley. **Kirkby Hardwick** takes its name from the same as the main place with the addition of Saxon *heord wic* or 'the shepherd's farm'. The Saxon *wic* always refers to a specialised farm, of which the vast majority are dairy farms. However, here we know the place was used for raising sheep, for it is well documented.

Nuncargate is a name of obvious Norse origins. Indeed it has its origins in three elements 'Nunna's *kiarr gata*', the personal name followed by 'marsh' and 'the way' or 'the road to Nunna's marsh'. **The Dumbles** is a name found only around the northern counties of the Midlands, a term referring to 'a wooded valley with a stream'. **Shoulder of Mutton Hill** is a somewhat imaginative name referring to the shape of the hill, although it would depend upon the observer's viewpoint.

If **Bentinck Town** seems to feature a familiar name you would be correct, for this is a reference to the name of the Dukes of Portland. Local families are also represented in places such as **Fishers Row** and **Heath's Cottages**. Representatives of each family are still resident in the town.

The **Duke of Wellington** is a fairly common pub name throughout the land. It recalls one of Britain's heroes, Arthur Wellesley (1769–1852). After a distinguished military career in India and Spain he famously defeated Napoleon's forces at the Battle of Waterloo. He later embarked on a political career and served as prime minister (1828–30) and then foreign secretary (1834–5). Known as the Iron Duke, his popularity remains as strong as ever, for only Nelson has more pubs in England named after him.

Kirklington

To anyone with even a little knowledge of place name origins this name would seem to be of Old Scandinavian beginnings. To suggest this without examining the early listings would be unwise – indeed the early forms are found as *Cyrlinstune* in 958, *Cherlinton* in 1086, and *Kirtlingtun* in 1220. These show the true origins to be a Saxon personal name with Old English *ing* + *tun*, giving 'the farmstead of the family or followers of Cyrtla'.

There can be few more delightful sounding names in the county than **Belle Eau Park**, which is particularly relevant for this literally means 'beautiful water'. These lands formed the estate around a moated hall, home to William de Bella-Aqua during the reign of Henry II and a tenant of the landholder, the Archbishop of York.

Kirton

Domesday's *Circeton* and *Kyrketona* from the twelfth century are the only records of note. This is clearly a name meaning 'village with a church'. However, the basis for this name is not quite as clear as it would seem. Even though Domesday can be inaccurate, as discussed in the introduction, this is not the reason for the obvious differences in the records of this name.

Initially this was an Old English name *cirice* + *tun*, however in later years the Scandinavian influence and pronunciation affected the evolution of the name to *kirkja* + *tun*. If the Saxon form had prevailed, the present place would probably have a sign showing this to be Chirchton or similiar.

Kneesall

Since this settlement was founded over a thousand years ago, the name has become contracted. Indeed, a quick look at the evolution of the name in early times shows that the present form has been affected by modern association of the pronunciation with that of the leg joint. Listed in 1086 as *Cheneshale*, in 1176 as *Cneshala*, by 1226 it was *Kneshal* and four years later *KeneshaleI*. The suffix here is Old English *halh* which follows a disputed personal name. However the most likely definition of Kneesall is '(place at) the nook of land of a man called Cyneheah'.

Two local farms have their origins in different tongues. **Baulk Farm** is from the Middle English *balke* telling of the 'farm on or near a ridge', while Old

Scandinavian *lundr* is 'farm in or near the grove' and appears on today's maps as **Lound Farm**.

Kneeton

A name with apparent similarities to the previous example. While this is also a personal name followed by an Old English element (here the very common *tun*), the individual cited is female. Recorded as *Cheniueton* in Domesday, as *Knivetun* in 1236, and as *Kenyueton* in 1292, this name began life as 'the farmstead of a woman called Cengifu'.

L

Lambley

Oddly, it is probably easier to see the meaning of this name in its modern form rather than the early records of *Lambeleia* in Domesday, *Lameleya* in 1191, and *Lameleia* in 1212. Undoubtedly this comes from the Old English *lamb* + *leah* or '(place at) the woodland clearing where lambs are pastured'.

Names such as this, which reveal a snapshot of life in Saxon England, are among the author's personal favourites. Furthermore, this name reveals more details than would be apparent. Firstly it tells us that the quality of the pasture was not ideal, otherwise the farm would have been raising cattle. Secondly the place must have been profitable for some time for, in order to have taken this name, the reason must have existed for a few years.

Locally we find **Harlow Wood**, a name of Saxon derivation from *hofer leah* and meaning 'the woodland clearing by the lump or hill'. **Bateman House** takes its name from the land of an administrative official, Gabriel Bateman, who was here in 1546. Finally there is **Wicketwood Hill**, which would suggest this is where materials were obtained to make the wickets or panels used to produce fences and screens. However, earlier it is recorded as *Wicked Wood*, which spoke of a place said to be haunted by supernatural beings and which should be avoided whenever possible. Both are equally plausible and, without further evidence, it is difficult to know which is correct – indeed, it is even possible that both explanations are true, although only one name would have been in use at any one time.

Laneham

Only two different records of this name are found, as *Lanum* in 1086 and *Lanun* exactly a century later. This is from Old English or Saxon *lanu* in its plural form of *lanum*, which has then evolved over the intervening centuries to what we would recognise as a place name. This comes from '(place at) the lanes'. Today there is little evidence of this being a particularly well-travelled region, thus we can only assume this referred more to commuters. Perhaps their goal was the other settlement here, known as **Church Laneham** for obvious reasons and possibly the central place of worship for this region.

At Laneham is the aptly named **North Beck**. It is exactly where it says in relation to the village, the basic name from Old Scandinavian *bekkr* 'stream'. This is a very common term in those regions of England which were influenced by the culture from Scandinavia, indeed in 1620 the stream is specifically referred to as the *Lanehame Becke*.

At Laneham is **The Ferry Boat Inn**, which stands within a few yards of the Trent. Public houses were natural centres for activity, in particular for transport. Nobody would ever question the idea of a horse being associated with a pub so why not a ferry service across the river?

Langar

A name of Old English origins from *lang* + *gara*. Listed as *Langare* in 1086 and in the modern form as early as 1163, this is clearly the 'the long gore or point of land'. As there is no mention of a settlement in the historical record, it seems likely that this name was coined for the area well before any settlement existed.

Langford

There are a number of places around the country with this name, mostly minor names, all of which come from 'the long ford'. However, the Nottinghamshire version is unique in that it has a different origin, as evidenced by records of *Landeforde* in 1086 and *Landeford* in 1201. Here the first element is uncertain. Possibly it is Old English *land* + *ford* where 'land' is used to describe 'the boundary or district ford'. However, there is a chance the first element here is a personal name and comes from 'Landa's ford'. That this place has not evolved to Landford is through the influence of the other Langfords.

Langold

A name first seen in 1246 as *Lanhalde* and quite clearly seen to come from Old English *lang* + *hald*. There is no precious metal to be found here unfortunately, for this name has its origins in 'the long shelter or place of refuge'. It is possible that this was originally a shelter for those in a hunting party, which existed well before any permanent settlement was founded here.

Laxton

A name found in Domesday as *Laxintune*, as *Laxintona* in 1200, and as *Laxinton* in 1198. This name comes from an Old English personal name with *inga* and *tun*, although it has been somewhat corrupted over the years and is now much shorter. Once it spoke of 'the farmstead of the family or followers of Leaxa'.

Within this village we find names such as **Knapeney Farm**, derived from Old English *cnapenhaga* meaning 'young men's enclosure' and despite the Saxon form does not have anything in common with Copenhagen. **Copthorn Farm** is quite easy to see as being from '(place at) the pollarded thorn'. Trees were pollarded by cutting the tops off at a height above that reached by browsers, thus encouraging the growth of straight fresh poles which were harvested and used in construction.

The name of **Straw Hall** is actually one of ridicule, not that we should consider any current buildings as likely to be toppled over by the slightest breeze, nor any of those previously built here. However, it does beg the question, was the place named before or after the story of *The Three Little Pigs*?

The local here is called the **Dovecote**, which was not named after the one which stands within the grounds – that was added much later. The most likely origin here is that there was once a dovecote on this site, although there is no evidence to support this.

Leake

In Domesday we find this name as *Leche*, by 1204 as *Lec*, in 1242 as *Lek*, and by 1242 there are two quite separate entries of *Westerlek* and *Estirlek*. This is a name of Old Scandinavian origins in *loekr* referring to the '(place at) the brook'. Quite clearly there are actually two places here, **East Leake** and **West Leake**, which are less than 2 miles apart.

Streets around East Leake have been named in honour of the people and events throughout its past. **Bateman Road** remembers long-serving rector the Revd John Bateman who was here from 1836 to 1882. From 1919 to 1944 the manager of the Marblaegis mine was one Captain Roulstone, the man who gave his name to **Roulstone Crescent**. A man who certainly deserved a road being named after him was Harry Carlton, who served on parish, rural district and county councils before giving his name to **Carlton Crescent**.

Other former residents gave their names to **Fisher Close** and **Moore Close**. Mr Fisher was a shepherd who died in 1648 and Mr Moore a yeoman who had died forty-five years earlier. Landowner John Hollis gave his name to **Hollis Meadow**, while the Oldershaw family farmed in the area for over 150 years, first as tenants and then as owners and are remembered in **Oldershaw Road**. John Bley (1674–1731) did as much for the village as anyone in its history, the benefactor giving his name to **Bley School** where Richard Hawley, geologist and schoolmaster, taught for forty-eight years and his achievements are marked by **Hawley Close**.

The Rope Walk is a very recent name, recalling the Ellis ropeworks which were here from 1974 to 1987. **Birch Lea** was built on a former Birch plantation.

Lenton

Even though there are only two early records of note of this place name, they are enough to confirm the origins. Indeed, a look at the map would be enough to suggest this was 'the farmstead on the River Leen' even before finding *Lentone* in 1086 and *Lemtona* in 1107.

Local names reflect former residents, including Thomas Allcock and Richard Cleaton, who were at **Allcock's Wood** and **Clayton's Bridge** in 1705 and 1690 respectively.

The White Hart at Lenton has what as been described as the finest wall sign in the country. It shows the stag in parkland, a badge of office around its neck and the curtain wall of Nottingham Castle in the background. The symbol was initially an heraldic one, used to denote Richard II. With so much water around, and with the popularity of water craft as a pub name, it is hardly suprising to find **The Boat** here.

Leverton

Actually there are two places here, **North Leverton** and **South Leverton**, which are less than a mile apart. Both are from the same beginnings, the suffix being Old English *tun*. This is thought to be a name describing the 'farmstead on the Legre', a Celtic river name which has defied all attempts at definition.

It is important not to assume anything when defining a place name, even when the origin seems obvious. For example there is a place here known as **Cowsland Farm**, a name which is not what it seems. Coming from the Old Scandinavian tongue, this has been much corrupted since it began life as 'the wood of a man named Kollr'. The element which has become 'land' started as the Norse term *lundr* meaning 'a wood'.

Linby

As disccused in the introduction, as a record for proper names, Domesday can be a little unreliable. Here the 1163 record of *Lindebi*, together with the modern form, is seen as a better clue to the origins than Domesday's *Lidebi*. Here we find the Old Scandinavian *lind* + *by*, telling us this is 'the farmstead where lime trees grow'.

Among the local names here are found **Hall Farm**, a corruption of *haga* or 'enclosure', and **Warkmill** which is listed in 1590 as *Walke Mill* and is a reference to a 'fulling mill'. Fulling is a process in the manufacture of cloth where the cloth was soaked to swell the fibres and give more depth to the cloth. It is most commonly seen today in the surname Walker, 'a fuller of cloth'.

Lindhurst

Listings of this name date from the thirteenth century and are plentiful. Records such as *Lyndehirst* in 1287, *Lyndhurst* in 1300, and *Lindehurst* in 1335 show the origin to be Saxon *lind + hyrst* or '(place at) the lime tree wood'.

Littleborough

A name recorded in Domesday as *Litelburg* and as *Lutilburg* in 1242. Even today's form of the name is self-explanatory as 'the little stronghold', from Old English *lytel + burh*.

Here we find the **Littleborough Bridge**, although this is a comparatively recent name. In 1330 it is recorded as *Staffordebrig*, which clearly comes from the Old English *staepford*. This reveals something of the place before any bridge was built here. It does not refer to a steep incline as it may seem, but speaks of 'the ford by the landing place'. Consequently we know that this point on the river has been of vital importance to the place for well over a thousand years.

Lound

A name of Old Scandinavian origin from *lundr* meaning '(place at) the small wood or grove'. It is a name only found in Suffolk, Lincolnshire and Nottinghamshire – this example was recorded as *Lund* in Domesday.

No matter what we might understand from the sound of **Neat Holm Road**, this is nothing to do with a well-kept residence but about as far from it as it possible to get. The only element of the three to mean what it seems is the last, *holmr* is an Old Scandinavian word for 'marsh meadow', while *neat* comes from the same tongue and refers to 'cattle'. Thus this should be seen as 'the road to or by the marshy land where cattle are grazed'.

Lowdham

Domesday records this place as *Ludham*, with later offerings of *Ludeham* from 1166, and as *Loudam* in 1258. This is an Old English personal name with the suffix *ham* telling of 'the homestead of a man called Hluda'.

Clearly, when defining many river and stream names, we find they are relevant to only a very small part of the overall length. Indeed most watercourses of more than a couple of miles in length would have had more than one name depending on who was speaking about it. For example, a river name describing it flowing alongside oaks would be unlikely to have those long-lived and magnificent trees along its banks for more than a one or two hundred yards at most. Thus before long we would find a name saying it flowed by aspen, beech, apple, or maybe some different local feature entirely. It can only have been when mapping the area, that one particular name for the river stuck. Which name would depend on who was doing the mapping and where. The **Cocker Beck** is one example of a local name which has become that of the whole length, even though it applies only to a very few yards. With its earliest surviving listing from 1235 as *le coker dike*, this is a name which is much older and comes from the British or pre-Roman tongue. Here we find the word *kukro* meaning 'crooked'. There is indeed a very sharp bend in the bed of the stream at Lowdham, the only bend which would stand out as anything different from others.

The pub here remembers history's most famous and important event of 1215. When King John was forced to sign the Magna Carta at Runnymede he set in motion a chain of events which reverberated down the centuries. It set out the constitution of the nation, reducing the effectiveness of the monarch and making parliament the real power. The pub is named the **Magna Charta**, not a spelling error, but simply an alternative.

M

Mansfield

The name of this town is recorded as *Mamesfelde* in 1086, *Mammesfelt* in 1093, *Mamefeld* in 1130, and *Mammefeld* in 1212. There is some uncertainty as to how the name came about, and thus just how to define it.

It may be that the name comes from 'open land by the River Maun', and that this is a Celtic river name from *mamm* 'the breast-shaped hill' together with Saxon *feld*. However, it could also be the case that the name comes directly from the hill itself – i.e. 'open land by the breast-shaped hill'. In this case the river would have taken its name from the place, a process known as back-formation. Without a sufficiently early record of the river name it is impossible to say; the earliest we have is *Mome* in 1235 and *Mone* in 1335, although of course the meaning is ostensibly the same.

A tributary of the Maun, which joins it here at Mansfield, is the **Cauldwell Brook**. It takes little imagination to see this as 'the cold stream' from Old English *cald wielle*. Once again the meaning was lost on later inhabitants which is why there is the recent and superfluous addition of 'Brook'.

Locally we find names such as **Dalesworth**, which comes from Old Scandinavian *deigju* 'dairy maid' and *storth* 'brushwood'. This odd combination appears to be referring to 'the home of the dairy maid among the brushwood'. The suffix here has clearly been corrupted by the Old English *worth*, although this tongue was the origin of **Hartrey Bridge** or 'the bridge of a woman named Haehoryth'.

Moorhaigh is derived from the Old English *mor* and *haga*, 'the (place at) the enclosure in swampy ground'. **Radmanthwaite** takes its name from three elements *hreod-mere-thveit* or 'the clearing by the reedy pool'. **Ravensdale Farm** comes from a Norse personal name and not the bird, although 'Hrafn's valley' features a name which comes from the word for the raven.

There are a number of individuals and families from across the centuries who have left a mark on the maps in and around Mansfield. **Dale Close** remembers Robert de Dale who was here in 1315, **Hall Barn** was home to John ad Aulum in

1327, **Walker's Pond** was on land belong to John Walker in 1560, Anne Thompson was resident at **Thompson's Grove** in 1566, and Alice Taylor lived near **Taylor's Plantation** in 1574. A map dated 1840 shows ownership by Richard Blythe and Abraham Sampson of places marked on modern maps as **Blythe's Barn** and **Sampson's Lane** respectively.

Streets around Mansfield remember life in the past around the town. **Mirehole Lane**, now renamed Sutton Lane as the original name sounded so undesirable, was well-named for it was difficult to travel along in the winter months. **Tenter Lane** recalls clothmaking, the tenter being the framework upon which the cloth was stretched to dry. **Padley Hill** comes from Middle English and, despite claims of being the haunt of footpads (highwaymen without a horse), it simply describes 'the footpath up the hill'. Archery practice was held in and around **Butt Close**, which was not from a personal name unlike **Spittlehouse Gate** which was a respected family in Mansfield's past.

Finally there is the name of **Toot Hill**, thought to be where fires were lit to celebrate the sacred time of the Beltane during the pre-Christian era. Flames would have been seen leaping high into the night on the eve of May Day, Midsummer Eve, and the night of 1 November. They were in celebration of the Celtic deity Taute, the equivalent of the Roman god Mercury.

Public houses in Mansfield include **The Nell Gwynn**, named after Eleanor Gwynn (1650–87). Much is made of the orange-seller who was also mistress to Charles II, however there was a notable gap bewtween her two 'careers'. It is true she sold oranges outside the theatre in Drury Lane, London, but only until the age of fifteen when she literally entered the theatre itself. A highly successful career as an actress followed, particularly in comedy where it was said her laugh was very real and highly infectious. Her delightful personality and friendly disposition made her popular with the men and she had many acquaintances. Her most famous liaison was with Charles II with whom she had two children. It has always been said the dying monarch's last words were 'Let not poor Nelly starve,' and his final wish was certainly complied with.

Another royal is honoured by **The Prince Charles**. However, no living royal appears on a pub sign therefore it has to be a character from history. The person in question is Charles Edward Stuart, known as Bonnie Prince Charlie, who attempted to restore the Jacobites to the three thrones of Britain. As history records, the 'Young Pretender' was spectacularly unsuccessful.

Finally there is the **Widow Frost**, a pub which stands close to the site of the former Masons Arms of which this woman was the first landlady. Just to confuse things further, prior to her arrival at the Masons, the pub was known as the Horse & Jockey.

Mansfield Woodhouse

It is often the case that place names with an additional second name to differentiate, and which are reasonably close to one other, began life as an outlying region of the original place. This does not seem to be the case with Mansfield Woodhouse which was recorded as *Wodehuse* in 1230 and as *Mamesfeld Wodehus* in 1280. Originally from the Old English or Saxon *wudu* + *hus*, it later took on the name of the larger settlement nearby and therefore should probably be defined as 'the woodland hamlet near Mansfield'.

The name of **Hind Car** tells us that this was once *deor kiarr* or 'the place at the marsh where deer are seen'. Not only are the wild creatures represented but former residents too. The family of Elizabeth Booth were at **Booth's Plantation** by 1732, while earlier still in 1639 Susan Cockes was just one of the family who gave their name to **Cox's Lane**, and by 1609 **Fletcher's Plantation** had taken its name from Michael Fletcher or one of his relations.

Pubs in the vicinity reflect the place surprisingly well. **The Four Ways** stands at the crossroads of the A60 and the A6075, and is a fairly common name for a pub at a junction. **The Coopers** is a public house named after the traditional name for barrel-makers.

Maplebeck

Even though the only record we have found is that of *Mapelbec* in 1086, there is no doubt this is a Saxon and Scandinavian hybrid. With a definition of '(the place at) the stream where maple trees grow', it is derived from Old English *mapel* and Old Scandinavian *bekkr*.

Markham

This name is undoubtedly derived from Old English *mearc* + *ham* 'the homestead on the boundary'. There are actually two places less than a mile apart, **East Markham** and **West Markham** which would have begun life as a single settlement. The records of *Marcham* in 1086, *Westmarcham* in 1086, and *Estmarcham* in 1191 confirm this.

The only uncertainty is the boundary itself. It is not a county boundary, for there are no historical records indicating that there was ever a boundary through here with Lincolnshire or Yorkshire. Thus we can only assume it must refer to a parish boundary, moreover the parish boundary of the original settlement at West Markham. There was never a boundary at **East Markham**, the name was simply taken there by those who founded the secondary settlement.

East Markham has a **College Farm**, not an actually seat of learning but held by one – the famous Trinity College, Cambridge. **Church Farm** is not directly attached to a church, nor is it adjacent to a place of worship. It was, however, held by one William super ecclesiam in 1327.

Marnham

As with the previous name there are two settlements here less than a mile apart; **High Marnham** and **Low Marnham**. These distinguishing additions are nothing to do with elevation above sea level, they refer to 'High' in the sense of having greater stature or importance. Indeed High Marnham is on the banks of the Trent, while its namesake is inland and higher up, albeit only marginally.

It almost seems to be stating the obvious to say the original place was High Marnham, it being recorded as *Marneham* in 1086 and *Marnaham* in 1175. This comes from a Saxon personal name followed by Old English *ham* giving 'the homestead of a man called Mearna'.

Mattersey

Written records from 1086 as *Madressei*, in 1200 as *Mareseia*, and in 1254 as *Mathersay* point to a beginning of '(the place at) the dry ground in wetland of a man called Maethhere'. This is from the Old English *eg* preceded by the personal name. This element is also seen as meaning an 'island'. Indeed, that is what is suggested here, that the settlement was founded on permanent dry ground in an area of wetland, or at least seasonal wetland.

Here is **Abbey Farm**, which stands on land belonging to the twelfth-century Gilbertine priory.

The ruins of Mattersey Priory which was established in 1185.

Maun, River

A Celtic river name discussed under Mansfield, probably coming from the hill near there.

Meden, River

A river which meets with the Maun to form the Idle, this is undoubtedly from the Old English *medune* meaning 'middle'. This is a comment on the character of the river; it is neither quick nor slow, large or small, deep or shallow, but literally average.

The River Meden near Budby.

Meering

A name found in early records as *Meringe* in 1086, *Merringge* in 1293, *Merynge* in 1368, *Meringe Chapell* in 1541, and *Meeringe* in 1627. This name describes the place as being 'the settlement of the dwellers by the mere', an apt enough name for it sits squarely in the midst of the flood plain of the River Test. Note the sixteenth-century listing also cites the name of the family who had had considerable influence in this manor for some time. However, the addition is quite late and it did not stick. As such additions are rarely found without good cause, such as a similar name nearby so added to differentiate, we might assume it was the result of a member of the Chappel family attempting to write his name into history.

Misson

A strange sounding English place name, for it seems to belong with another element. Here is another Old English name from *mos* meaning 'mossy, marshy'. Records of *Misne* in 1086, *Misun* in 1212, *Misene* in 1228, and *Miseneya* in 1247 show this has identical origins to Muizen in Belgium and Mijsen in the Netherlands. Certainly the name is highly applicable to all three places.

The local map records the name of **Norwith Hill**. This comes from an Old Scandinavian word *vithr* meaning 'wood', thus this is 'north wood hill'.

Misterton

Perhaps we should be thankful for the record from 1166 as *Mistertona*, for if all we had to work with was Domesday's *Ministretone* the origin may be misunderstood. Along with its namesake in nearby Leicestershire, this name comes from Old English *mynster* + *tun* and means 'the farmstead belonging to the church or monastery'.

This is almost as far north as we can get without leaving the county. Here is **Bycarrs Dike**, a name recorded in Domesday as *Bigredic* and in 1155 as *Bichersdic*. We are fairly certain this name comes from Old Scandinavian *by carr* 'the village marsh'. The addition refers to a specially dug ditch. This was a channel or canal dug to connect the rivers Idle and Trent and provided a welcome shortcut between the two. There is no actual evidence of a ditch having been dug alongside the canal, so perhaps the ditch is the canal or channel itself and the marsh referred to was named as such well before the shortcut was dug. This is an example of a name's origin being known but the message is uncertain.

Other local examples include **Misterton Carr**, **Carr Farm** and **North Carr Farm** all of which are defined when we know the common element *kiarr* is the Old Scandinavian word for fenland. Indeed the fen in question once extended across into neighbouring Yorkshire and Lincolnshire. There is also a **Carr Ings**, which has the second element from *eng* and refers to 'low-lying grassland' in fenland.

Listed in 1286 as *Cattehale*, **Cattle Farm** has the second element *healh*, an Old English word describing a 'corner of land'. Thus this was 'the nook where wild cats were seen'. Other animals were found at the place known in Old English as *corna leah* 'the clearing frequented by cranes or heron' and today known as **Cornley**.

Debdhill Farm and **Debd Hill** have that unusual first element. Indeed it is an unusual hill for it is only a maxiumum of 49ft 3in above the surrounding land, yet is the only feature in a predominantly featureless landscape. In fact it seems this nature of the landscape is the basis for a name which, at first glance, seems to be almost a typographical error. It is thought this name refers, albeit laughingly, to the '(place at) the deep dale'.

There is also the rather unusual name of **Misterton Soss**. The latter element here is a term which originated in this part of the country. It is a Middle English term used to describe a 'mess, slop, puddle, dirty water', although the dialect word has fallen out of general use.

Muskham

There are two places in Nottinghamshire with this name, about a mile apart, **North Muskham** and **South Muskham** – with obvious reasons for the additions. Listings of the two date back as far as Domesday when they appear as simply *Muscham* with the alternative of *Nordmuschum*. We should be careful of suggesting this implies that

South Muskham was the original, it may simply be that Domesday is (once again) inaccurate. Indeed later records show these places as *Muscampe* in 1155, *Muscamp* in 1166 and *Sutmuscham* in 1242.

There have been suggestions that these names come from Old English *mus* + *ham*, which would give us 'the mouse-infested place'. However, this does not stand up to scrutiny. While the likelihood is that this was once one settlement which later founded a second outlying place to live, there are several possible reasons for this, lack of space being the obvious. More often it began life as a temporary farming settlement, either as a storage facility for crops, or to accommodate the farmers and/ or their livestock. In such examples it is not uncommon for the original name to be transferred to the overspill settlement. Even though the vast majority of names are coined by their neighbours, the residents simply called the place 'home', it seems unlikely they would have used the same name for the new place, and even less likely that the name would be applicable for they certainly would not want to take the mice with them!

Yet these early forms certainly point to something similar. Therefore this is probably a personal name, or more correctly a nickname, giving 'the homestead of a man called Musca'.

In North Muskham there is a place called **Belfield** which is an enclosure named after a former tenant, William Bell who was here in 1689. South Muskham features the name of a previous resident too, William Chouler being at **Choulers Gorse** in 1850. There is also a field name, **Dumble Plantation**, a word used to describe 'a wooded valley with a stream'.

N

Nether Langwith

A name which is of Old Scandinavian origins, from *langr* + *vath* and speaking of the '(place at) the long ford'. It must be understood that the term 'long' is more likely to have implied great width of the ford rather than width of the river, for the broader the river invariably means deeper and a stronger current making any crossing difficult. The addition of Nether is to distinguish this place's location downstream from Upper Langwith, which is not mentioned in this book because it is in Derbyshire.

Two local names of interest here, one being **Cockshut Lane** which refers to 'a corner of land into which woodcock are driven' and provides a snapshot of life in Saxon times when this bird was a highly prized food source. We also find **Deadman's Grave** which, despite what local stories would suggest, should end in 'grove'. Obviously this second element has been affected by the first; it is correct but does not refer to a burial point but is a family name.

It was soon realised that the pub sign offered the opportunity for some imaginative advertising. Thus names were created almost as advertising slogans, names which could be nothing other than pubs such as the **Jug and Glass**.

Newark on Trent

Clearly this place takes its suffix from the county's most prominent watercourse. As dicussed under its own entry this name means 'trespasser' i.e. 'liable to flood'.

The basic place name requires the addition for there is an identical name in Peterborough, although there is some 40 miles between them. This name is derived from old English *niwe* + *weorc* 'the new fortification', with records of *Newercha* in 1054, *Niweweorce* in 1075, and *Newerche* in Domesday.

Street names in a town such as Newark will always reflect the history of the place. What is represented by each name depends largely on the era from which it is taken.

The oldest names come from the landscape, the more recent from individuals, especially those who were instrumental in the major building expansions with the onset of the Industrial Revolution, as the nation went from agricultural- to manufacturing-based economy with amazing speed.

Examples locally include **Appleton Gate** or 'the road by the orchard'. **Bargate** is a fairly common name in old towns, it refers to 'the road closed by a bar' and possibly the site of a toll station. A bede house or a charitable house for the poor and sick was located in **Bede House Lane**. Inmates were encouraged to pray for the soul of the founder of the house, thus providing their beneficiary with a good reputation for when his or her time came to enter the afterlife, while at the same time ensuring they received the best care available to them in return.

Boar Lane seems unlikely to have anything to do with the animal; it is thought to have been the name of an inn which once stood here, itself taking its name from the crest of a landowner or sponsor. **Kirkgate** is a Scandinavian-influenced 'church street'. **Lombard Street** tells us it is 'the street of the potters'. However, the street in Newark is not named after any potters but has been copied from the the street

Newark Castle as viewed across the Trent.

in London. **Stodmare Street** is documented as being where a stud mare was stabled and offered for selective breeding, if the price was right.

Three names here, clearly linked, proved difficult to define for some time. That was until the rarely used Dutch word *schans*, referring to a 'small fort', was dicovered. In Nottinghamshire there were temporary fortifications built during the English Civil War. These appear on today's maps as **Sconce Hills**, **King's Sconce** and **Queen's Sconce**.

Near the Queen's Sconce bubbles forth a spring, known as St Catherine's Well. It has given rise to a fourteenth-century tale of murder, infidelity, chivalry, visions and a miraculous cure by the waters of the well. The actual tale differs depending upon who is telling it and when. However, three characters remain constant, other than the woman herself, and they are remembered in the names of the streets named **Bevercotes**, **Saucemere** and **de Caldwell**.

Kings Road was known as Appleton Close until the sale of Crown lands in 1836 meant the road could be widened and thus renamed. **Stephen Road** is named after King Stephen, who had close associations with Newark Castle. Another well-known figure from English history is Cardinal Wolsey, who gave a name to **Wolsey Road**. In truth the most powerful man in England at one time did not have any direct association with the town, but his great friends and benefactors Robert Browne and Dr Magnus did.

Harcourt Street was named by an unknown someone who wished to honour the man who was Gladstone's right-hand through much of his long political career, namely one William George Granville Venables Vernon Harcourt. The housing estate developed by Mr T. Bailey of nearby Lenton gave **Lenton Terrace** its name, while Mr Dennis Lilley's involvement in another development gave rise to **Lilley's Row**. The houses around **Brewster's Yard** were built by John Brewster, who lived in nearby **Victoria Street**, named after the monarch of the day.

Developer Thomas Smith left monies in his will to build houses in **Wright Street**, named by the firm of solicitors who were executors of the estate. **Fleming Drive** remembers the contribution of Alan Fleming, a local merchant who founded the Chapel of Corpus Christi before his death in 1361. **Cotton Square** was purpose built by the owners of the cotton mill so their employees would not only be on hand but also returning some of their hard-earned money in rent.

Perhaps the most unexpected names in the town also have a most unusual etymology. The region around **China Place** was owned by a Mr Toder. The man had a few strings to his bow, including a retail business in the square and a stall in the market where he personally sold china. He friends gave him the nickname 'China Pot', which was then transferred to the street.

The **Sawmill** public house stands on the site of Thomas Smith's timber yard, thus has a most appropriate name. **The White Swan** is often thought to be heraldic and yet, although it does feature in the coat of arms of the Vintners' Company, it more often refers to the bird seen on the local pond or river. **The Malt Shovel** is a common name for a pub and an early one. A specially shaped tool for turning the barley grain, it would have been displayed as the actual sign – much cheaper than painting it.

It would not seem unusual to find the **Castle and Falcon** referring to the upper classes. However, it refers very specifically to one royal, the one wife of Henry VIII who managed to survive him, Catherine Parr. **The Bridge** most often tells us this is where a river or canal is crossed although the sign depicts a steam engine so clearly that this is obviously a reference to the railway. **The Famous Old Post Office** is a pub which, true to its name, is a part of the same building which served as the old post office.

The **Sir John Ardene** may seriously challenge even those with some local knowledge. The gentleman in question lived and/or worked in Newark and was a doctor whose reputation was enhanced by his work in the study and treatment of haemorrhoids. It is uncertain if this was the reason for his knighthood.

Newstead

A name not seen until the twelfth century as *Novus Locus* and then as *Newstede* in 1302. This is undoubtedly from Old English *niwe* + *stede* or 'the new monastic site'. It is tempting to suggest this was 'new' in comparison with Kirkby in Ashfield, however there is no reason to believe it is this place any more than Felley Priory or Newstead Abbey.

Locally are found a number of names taken from a variety of sources. **Hoppinghill Farm** can still be seen to refer to 'the place where hops are grown', as can 'the goose-frequented ford' in **Gosford Plantation**. However, the name of **Gibbetdale Wood** has nothing to do with gallows, it is simply a corrupted form of 'Gilbert quarry', the personal name almost certainly a family name.

Normanton on Soar

As discussed in the following entry, the name of Normanton refers to 'the farmstead of the Norsemen'. Here the addition is the River Soar, a name from the Celtic languages meaning simply 'the flowing one'.

Normanton-on-Trent

The basic name here is a fairly common one around the area where the Scandinavian influence was strong. Thus it is no surprise that the name describes 'the farmstead of the Norsemen'.

Several times in this book it has been said that the name of a place is rarely given by the inhabitants but normally by a neighbouring settlement. The early records of this name not only show this to be the case, but also gives an indication of which neighbours gave the name. Domesday records the name as *Normentone* in 1086, from a record dated 1272 we find *Normanton super Trentam* which is the same as today. Fifteen years later in 1287 the name is recorded as *Normanton juxta Weston*, and in 1343 *Normanton juxta Gresthorp*. All these names, 'on Trent', 'near Weston', and 'near Gresthorp', are correct depending upon the observer's viewpoint.

There is an unusual field name here, one that merits a little attention. Not that the name of **Brotts** is difficult to see coming from Old Scandinavian *brot* meaning 'piece, fragment (of land)', it is simply very rare to find this used as a place name.

Normanton on the Wolds

As with the previous entries, the name is associated with a region where Scandinavian influence was strong. Meaning 'the farmstead of the Norsemen', the addition is found only in the region of Nottinghamshire and its neighbouring counties of Leicestersire, Lincolnshire and Yorkshire. The term is used to refer to upland region and is very specific in its meaning. It comes from the Old English *wald* or 'high former forested land, now mostly cleared'.

Norton

A very common place name indeed, always from Saxon meaning 'the northern farmstead'. The surprising thing about this place north of Cuckney is that it has no second distinguishing element.

Locally we find **Hatfield Grange** or 'the heath of open land', and **Milnthorpe** 'the outlying farmstead with a mill'.

Norton's ornate village sign

Norwell

Listed in Domesday as *Nortwelle* it appears as the modern form as early as 1167. This name is derived from Old English *north* + *wella*, predictably the '(place at) the northern stream'.

Locally we find **Palis Hall** (sometimes recorded as Palace Hall), which comes from the Old French *palis* or *paleis* speaking of a 'palisade' or 'paling', both a reference to the defensive fencing around the hall. **Flags Farm** refers to the 'flaggy belt of sandstone' running through the farm. **Swinnis Villa** is a name which was originally *swin haga*, 'the swine enclosure'. However, the name of 'Villa' is a corruption of Old Scandinavian *vro* meaning 'corner of land'.

Nottingham

The main settlement and administrative centre of the county is found as early as the late ninth century as *Snotengaham*, while Domesdays' *Snotingeham* is remarkably close to the original Saxon *Snot* + *inga* + *ham*. The middle element of *inga* is only found in place names when it follows a personal name, telling of 'the people or followers of . . .'. It is tempting to think of the named individual as a tribal leader or chieftain. However, it is more likely to have been a tribute to an earlier prominent figure – indeed the man himself may never have seen the place which bears his name. Nottingham takes its origins from 'the homestead of Snot's people'.

Sometimes there are suggestions that the earlier forms of the name are resurrected. Somehow I doubt if there will be many voices heard requesting that that the initial 'S', which was lost in the twelfth century owing to Norman influence, be reinstated!

From the Old Scandinavian *bekkr* meaning simply 'stream' is the name of **The Beck**. This small tributary of the Trent is recorded as *Bec* 1230 and *le Bek* 1362. Today the stream is covered and forms part of the city's sewers. Another simple stream name is that of the **River Leen**. Recorded as *Liene* in about 1200, *Lene* in 1218, and *Leen* in 1232, it comes from the Old English *lei*, literally 'to flow' but used to convey the message that this tributary of the Trent was not standing water.

The **Tottle Brook** runs down from **Bramcote Ridge** – 'the cottages among the broom' – into the valley to join the Trent at Lenton. This stream name comes from an alternative name for the hill. From *tote-hill* this is 'the look out hill', although it is not found until 1825.

It cannot have gone unnoticed that while we have bridges named after every major town or city, the bridge at Nottingham is named after the river. The reason is simple; when **Trent Bridge** was first built the nearest part of the city was a mile away. Edward the Elder captured Nottingham in 924 and built the first bridge. Piers of stone supported a wooden platform and superstructure. It was in use until 1156, when it was replaced under the orders of Henry II, and was of great importance as it was the last to cross the Trent before it reached the sea many miles away.

Interestingly the locals always refer to the bridge in the plural, and there is no smoke without fire, so there is almost certainly some reason for this seeming error. There are two equally plausible suggestions for 'The Bridges'. When the bridge was first built on the present site it ran alongside the former crossing point, which remained open until the new bridge had been completed. Obviously this was not accomplished overnight, therefore for some time there would indeed have been two bridges. The second suggestion puts the bridges in series, not in parallel, meaning what appeared to be one bridge over the marshy flood plain and river was, in reality, two bridges of separate construction, one after the other.

Another bridge has given rise to the name of **Chainey Flash**. Two pools were crossed by a weir, small boats wanting to descend from one to the other were 'flashed' over the drop using small waves of water. The bridges across here were closed to traffic unless the river was in full flood, access being denied by the chain fastened across each end. Together the two terms formed the name.

Fishpond Drive was constructed on the area of one of the old fishponds of Nottingham Castle. Over the years the ponds, having out lived their usefulness, silted up and were eventually used to take the soil removed from a nearby building. The building in question was the barracks erected in 1791 in what is now Barrack Lane.

Once an important position in any community, pinders of Nottingham even had a home allotted to them. When farming was small-scale and most livestock grazed on communal land, it was not as easy for owners to ensure their animals did not stray. Having livestock wandering around dining on the vegetable patch was clearly unacceptable and a member of the community was appointed as pinder to round up the strays and keep them until the requisite fine was paid. This man was paid out of the fines and was given a house, giving the names of **Pinders Street** and **Pinders House Road**.

Burton's Alms Houses were established in 1859 by Miss Ann Burton from the fortune left to her by her father who had been a prosperous saddler. **Redcliffe Road** was formerly known as Red Lane. Both refer to its red clay base which, when coupled with the challenging gradient, made the road impassable for much of the year. **Island Street** is named from being the lane through marshland.

Red Lion Street was named such in 1905, previously it had been called Narrow Marsh, 'narrow' describing the path through it and not the wetlands themselves. It ran between the Leen and St Mary's cliff and, in 1315, was known by the grander sounding *Parvus Mariscus*. However, by the end of the ninth century it had earned a reputation for being a place of hoodlums and undesirables. This was a major factor in the decision to change the name, which was a pity considering its importance in the history of the region. Indeed with the narrow causeway it would have been unlikely anyone would have given the place a second glance as a potential home.

Nottingham's splendid council offices with the modern wheel and tram lines in front.

A couple of reminders of the leather tanning industry are found in **Knob Yard** and **Vat Yard**. The latter is, predictably, where the hides were processed in the tanning vats. The 'knob' is a term applied to the cut-offs from the hides which were considered waste. Another trade is marked by **Maltmill Lane** which led down to one of the ancient mills on the River Leen.

Butlers Court remembers Mistress Butler, a tenant of this place from possibly before 1769, until her death at the age of ninety-two some years later. Another resident who has left his name on the landscape is George Malyne who lived near **Malin Hill** in 1303.

In more recent times roads have been named **Peach Street**, **Plum Street**, **Pear Street** and **Currant Street** – the last example is not a typographical error. All were built on land formerly owned by the Gregory family. Apparently the family really enjoyed their fruit.

Finally, two individuals whose eccentric behaviour certainly warranted them being immortalised in the sign showing the name of the place where they lived. **Darker's Court** is named after an old miser, Thomas Darker, who was here in 1847. He became increasingly deranged, refusing to venture out of his single room other than to visit a nearby well under the cover of darkness. He repelled all who attempted to contact him, even his own brother was threatened with a gun when he broke into the room. Eventually Darker went completely mad and, failing to treat a fever, he died. Later a search of his room revealed a large cache of gold and silver coins.

Back to what was then still known as Narrow Marsh for our final Nottingham street tale. For seventy-six years James Hutchinson had been a framework knitter working from his home, for the last twenty years the frame never left his window, nor did his seat move from alongside it. He died in 1813. During his whole life he never ventured more than 7 miles from his home in Nottingham. He also had some strange drinking habits. He was fond of proclaiming he had never even tasted tea and, most unusually for a time when water was considered unsafe to drink, drank no ale for almost the last twenty years of his life.

His diet was even stranger. In the same window as he worked were lined up fourteen vessels, each containing a pennyworth of milk which he had purchased on fourteen consecutive days. Each day he would consume the oldest of the milk, the more sour and clotted it was, the more he liked it. During the warmer months the clotted milk in the window would often become too hard to swallow, he referred to this as 'cheesecake' and would boil it in order to make it liquid, and therefore drinkable once more.

Such unusual behaviour did not affect him unduly. He lived until he was ninety-three, leaving at least thirty descendants. For the meals alone he surely merited the name of **Hutchinson Green**.

The Bentinck Hotel recalls the family who, over a number of generations, have provided a prime minister, a Governor of India and the Dukes of Portland. **The Colonel Burnaby** remembers the nineteenth-century British soldier and adventurer. Another military figure who later turned his hand to politics was **Sir Charles Napier**. This naval leader helped cement relations with foreign powers by aiding them in their endeavours. **Sir John Borlase Warren** also attained the rank of admiral, and later represented the people in the House of Commons. He was born in Stapleford in 1753.

Edmund Kean was an actor who appeared in Nottingham playing the title role in *Hamlet*, alongside his wife. He has been immortalised in **The Keans Head**. **The John Barleycorn** does not remember an actual person but is a term referring to the product, be it beer, ale or any alcoholic beverage made from malt. It is referred to in song and by some of the most respected literary figures, including Nathaniel Hawthorne, Sir Walter Scott and Robert Burns. One more recently named pub is the **Bread and Bitter** which refers to the present building (bitter) and its former use as a bakery (bread).

Sometimes defining a name gives us a glimpse of the past. A place name can be so descriptive as to give an instant mental image of the place when it was so named. The **Jolly Higglers** tells us something of the customers in early days. The term 'higgler' refers to the wandering souls who bought smaller items from farms, such as dairy produce and poultry, bringing them to barter in the town's market. More often than not they would exchange goods and no money would change hands until they returned to the country and sold them there. The term has evolved to be 'haggle' in modern times. A change of vowel like this is not unusual. Whether buying or selling they drove the hardest of bargains in order to earn a profit, thus enabling them to enjoy a drink in the aptly-named establishment.

While the **Up and Under** might sound a contradiction to those who have never heard the expression before, the rugby fraternity will recognise it instantly. This describes when the ball is hoofed 'up' high into the air and behind the forward line of the opponents, while your team attempt to get 'under' the dropping ball, thus retaining possession. The location of the **Via Fossa** next to the water is rather unexpected, for the name is Latin for the famous Roman road the Fosse Way. Indeed the name even tells us it is a Roman road for it was (then) unique in having a drainage ditch alongside; the word *fossa* means 'ditch'.

The **Vat and Fiddle** employs a play on words. It stands just around the corner from the local office where VAT returns are examined, indeed the sign of both places are very similar. There is also the similarity with the Cat and Fiddle and in the world of taxation the 'fiddle' is not a stringed intstrument. The same wordplay is found at the **Stick and Pitcher**, the pitcher obviously being the large jug in which drink is served. However, here it may also be a sporting term, a reference to the pitches outside where hockey is played, hence the stick. Furthermore there is a small bar downstairs called the **Short Corner**, not only a hockey term but also where 'shorts' can be ordered.

The most famous pub in Nottingham has to be **Ye Olde Trip To Jerusalem**, indeed it must rank among the most famous in the country. It is unique in having been hollowed out of the rock on which Nottingham Castle stands. Outside, the date AD 1189 appears which for a long time suggested a link with the Crusades. However, there is a clue in the name itself which tells us this cannot be the case. The word 'trip' was not in use before the fourteenth or fifteenth centuries. Furthermore it has always been used to describe a journey which took little time. If this was the case here the name would be more fitting as the Trek to Jerusalem. It seems these caves and tunnels were used as a brewhouse, but not before the seventeenth century. Furthermore no mention of a pub of this or any other name is found until the eighteenth century. Surely such a rare and unusual place would have attracted many mentions and some would invariably have survived if this had been used as an inn prior to this. Thus the name can only have been created to suggest some association with the Crusades, possibly from a tale once told locally.

Nottinghamshire

The city of Nottingham (see previous entry) gave its name to the county. It was in the eleventh century that the first record of Nottinghamshire is found. The addition comes from the Saxon *scir* or 'shire' simply referring to a 'district', in this instance for administrative purposes.

Nuthall

Here is an Old English name from *hnutu* and *halh* giving '(place at) the nook of land where nut trees grow'. Records of this place go back to the eleventh century with Domesday's *Nutehale* and as *Notehal* in 1194.

The parish includes names such as **Hempshill Farm**, which took its name from the settlement here which was '(the place) at Hemede's hill'. Maps from 1684 and 1716 showed residents Thomas Carter and Joan Sellers respectively, who gave their names to **Carter's Wood** and **Seller's Wood**. It comes as little surprise to find **Verge Wood** stands on the boundary at the eastern end of the parish.

O

Ollerton

Domesday records this place as *Alretun* which, with the unreliability of the great work as discussed in the introduction, may well be seen to be an error if it were not for the record of *Alreton* from 1176. Indeed a little local knowledge also helps to define this name. These old forms are not erroneous, they represent Old English *alor* + *tun* or 'the farmstead where alder trees grow'. That the name has evolved to 'Oller-' rather than 'Alder-' is due to that element being pronounced as *owler* in many dialects around Nottinghamshire and its adjoining counties.

The Old Mill in the background, behind this road sign in Ollerton.

Within the town are two thoroughfares, both having somewhat unusual names. **Brescar Lane** comes from the Old Scandinavian *beiskr* meaning 'bitter'. While the meaning is certain, the suggestion is a little vague, although the most likely explanation is that the vegetation here produced a distinctive bitter taste. There is also **Tor Lane**, which clearly refers to a hill, not a particularly large hill but certainly a steep one.

The pub name of the **Snooty Fox** is becoming more common. The fox has been symbolic of wisdom and cunning, a successful animal equally at home in the country and in the town. This has made the fox ideal for a pub name, while also being instantly recognisable on the sign. Many pubs took a second element to differentiate, while sign painters became more imaginative with their depiction of the fox. Thus it appears in various guises, particularly standing on its hind legs dressed as a dandy, often wearing top hat and monocle. It was a simple step to see the creature as being upper-crust, even appearing to look down on others, thus 'snooty', which also gives the suggestion the pub is above others.

Above, left: *Nineteenth-century water bowser for the refill of steam-powered engines at Ollerton.*

Above, right: *Ollerton church.*

The River Maun at Ollerton.

Ompton

A name recorded as *Almuntone* in 1086 and as *Almeton* in 1182, here is a Saxon personal name with Old English *tun*. This place was originally 'Alhmund's farmstead'. Here we also find **Flash Lane** which comes from the Middle English *flasshe* meaning 'pool or marshy place'.

Ordsall

A name recorded as *Ordeshale* in 1086, *Hordesal* in 1254, and *Ortsall* in 1557, can only have one origin as 'Ord's nook of land'.

Orston

With records such as *Oschinstone* in 1086, *Oschintona* in 1093, *Oschintuna* in 1146, *Oskinton* in 1198, and exactly as the modern form by 1254, we can see this name has become much shortened over time. Although there is a little uncertainty in the Saxon personal name, it is clearly followed by Old English *inga* + *tun*, giving us 'farmstead of the family or followers of Osica'.

Ossington

If we were looking for examples of how identical names could evolve quite differently, Ossington and the previous name of Orston are quite perfect. Compare Ossington's Domesday listing of *Oschintone* in 1086, then compare *Oscintone* in 1167 and *Oscington* in 1275 and you will begin to see how the two diverged. The meaning of both is identical as 'the farmstead of the family or followers of Osica'. However it should not be thought they refer to the same person for the two settlements are around 20 miles apart and would probably have not even been aware of the existence of the other.

There is a field name here, **Park Lidget**, which is derived from *hlidgeat* 'the swing gate'.

Owthorpe

Listings of this name are found as *Ovetorp* in 1086, *Uuetorp* in 1194, and *Uuethorp* in 1230. While the meaning is understood, the exact personal name involved depends largely upon his ancestry. While the suffix is undoubtedly Old Scandinavian *thorp* the first element may be an Old English personal name, Ufa. Hence this place began life as 'the outlying farmstead of Ufi or Ufa'.

Minor names in the parish have origins ranging from before the time of the Normans right up to the twentieth century and **Spencer's Bridge**. While there are still representatives of that name in the village it is unknown if they are related to the individual concerned. Further back in history **Mackley's Bridge** and **Wild's Bridge** were named after John Mackley and Sarah Wild in 1762 and 1766 respectively.

As mentioned there is an earlier name dating from Saxon times. The name of **Herrywell Lane** most certainly comes from Old English *here weg* meaning 'army road'. Clearly there was some knowledge of an army being associated with this route, although just what that association was is unclear.

Oxton

Even if we were unaware of Domesday's entry as *Oxetune* we would be fairly certain of the origins of this name for the modern form virtually tells us. Here the Old English elements of *oxa* and *tun* combine to tell us this was 'the farmstead where oxen were kept'.

P

Papplewick

With listings of this name as *Papleuuic* in 1086, as *Papelwic* in 1212, and *Papelwyc* in 1230, we have no doubt as to the origins of this name. Here are two Old English elements *papol* and *wic*, which tells us this was 'the specialised farm on pebbly ground'. Normally a Saxon *wic* or 'specialised farm' would refer to the rearing of a dairy herd. However, while not impossible, a stony or pebbly soil would not seem to fit with decent pasture, or be particularly good for the cloven hooves of cattle. Thus it is likely that this farm specialised in another commodity, maybe something such as bees, for honey was a valuable and much sought-after food item. Furthermore it requires the minimum of man hours. The bees do all the work. All that is required is collection and packaging.

Stankerhill is a local name derived from the elements *stan* + *kiarr*, giving us 'the hill by the stony marsh'. This seems a little contradictory, stony marshland is an odd combination, and may well tell us there has been human intervention. Coming from the Old English *barre* + *ac* is a name meaning 'the barrier by the oaks', and probably tells us that **The Barracks** was once where a gate stood, indeed it may well have been a toll gate. At first Barracks may have suggested a military origin yet nothing could be further from the truth, unlike the names of **Howe Plantation** and **Vincent Plantation**. The individuals named are Earl Howe and Earl St Vincent, their names taken in honour of the eighteenth-century naval victories of Admiral Sir Richard Howe and Admiral Sir John Jervis respectively.

The Griffins Head here features the fabled beast, said to be a cross between a lion and an eagle. To be considered as having the attributes of two of the most respected of animals, this made it a favourite choice in heraldry. With so many coats of arms having this element, it is difficult to know what the link is. Furthermore, the symbol was often chosen to represent families called Griffin when they were connected with the establishment.

Plumtree Village sign.

Plumtree

Domesday almost got this place name right with *Pluntre*, however the modern form is perfect for this really is '(the place at) the plumtree'. This is a Saxon name and comes from their Old English language as *plum* + *treow*.

Poulter, River

A river which is a tributary of the Idle. Listed in 1589 as both *Paltr* and *Palter*, this is clearly a case of the river taking its name from the village of Palterton in neighbouring Derbyshire. Unfortunately this name has never been defined with any certainty, only the suffix of *tun* 'farmstead' is unquestioned. It has been suggested the first element may be a combination of Old English *pall* 'ledge' and *torr* 'hill' yet, although the possibility cannot be denied, the two elements together is otherwise unknown. However, the river has not always been recorded under this name. In 1707 it is called the *Clumber River*. Along its course the river has been dammed to create ornamental pools for what are now National Trust properties such as Clumber Park. It seems likely that this name came from the river itself, a British or Celtic name identical in origin to Clun, Colne and Calne. Unfortunately, once again, this name is difficult to tie down. Suggestions of being related to Latin *calare* and Welsh *ceiliog*, understood to describe a 'roaring river', may have fitted once, but without further and earlier evidence this is purely speculation.

R

Radcliffe-on-Trent

A name found in other places, the closest is a part of Greater Manchester, although more often found as a minor name. This place was recorded as *Radeclive* in 1086 and as *Radeclyf super Trent* in 1291. Along with every other Radcliffe (also Ratcliffe and Redclive) this comes from Old English *read* + *clif* '(the place at) the red cliff or bank'.

As this name is so common an addition is to be expected. Here is the name of the county's major watercourse, the origins of which are discussed under its own entry.

Two local names of interest are **Parr's Barn Farm**, a reference to a Margaret Parr who was here in 1633. **Lamcote House** is a place built on land where, early in the history of the village, 'lamb cotes or pens' were used to keep the livestock safe.

Local pubs include the **Black Lion**, an heraldic emblem which can be traced back to Queen Philippa of Hainault, wife of Edward III. There is nothing to suggest a direct link between the place and the queen, however such emblems are passed down through a lineage and properties and this is how the place got its name. It is likely to have been taken from the coat of arms of the owner of the land or the pub. **The Royal Oak** is the second most popular pub name in the country, remembering the escape of Charles II and his aide from the Battle of Worcester. Pursued by the enemy they hid in the Boscobel Oak, near Shifnal in Shropshire. The sign was used to show support for the monarchy. The close proximity of one of the country's main rivers made the naming of the **Trent Inn** almost inevitable.

Radford

Listings of this name date from Domesday as *Redeford*, in 1108 as *Radeford*, and in 1209 as *Radford*. This is from the Old English *read* giving 'the red ford'. Normally this would be thought of as being from 'the reed or reedy ford', however there is a very red sandstone here.

At Radcliffe-on-Trent a road name indicates early trades, this being a reference to cloth making.

Minor names found here include **Aspley Hall**, built on what was once 'the clearing of the aspen trees'. **Hyson Green** seemed an interesting name until it was discovered on an early map. The modern form is a rather corrupted version of the original 'high sands', while 'green' is common to many villages.

At Radford is the **Marquis of Lorne** public house, which remembers John George Edward Henry Douglas Sutherland Campbell (1845–1920). A member of parliament for Strathclyde, he was Governor-General of Canada from 1878 to 1883. In 1871 he married Princess Louise, the fourth daughter of Queen Victoria.

Ragnall

This is an example of a hybrid name, where an Old Scandinavian personal name precedes the Old English *hyll*. Records of *Ragenehil* in Domesday, *Raghenehull* in 1230, and as *Ragenhil* in 1242, enable us to define this name as 'Ragni's place at or near the hill'.

Near here is **Whimpton Moor**, a place recorded as *Wimentun* in 1086, *Wimuntton* in 1168, *Wimpton* in 1232, and *Wympton* in 1280. Clearly today's version is a somewhat corrupted version from the original 'Wigmund's settlement'.

Rainworth

The records of *Rayngwath* in 1280 and *Reynewathford* in 1300 are somewhat overly complicated and help little in trying to tie down the first element here. There is no doubt this is of Old Scandinavian origins. However, whether this is *hreinn + vath* '(the place at) the clean ford' or *rein + vath* '(the place at) the boundary ford' is unclear.

Recorded in about 1650 as *the river Raynwith*, the local watercourse known as **Rainworth Water** quite obviously takes its name from the place. Indeed this back-formation, as it is known, is also seen in the previous name. For in 1540 it is listed as the *Rufford streame*, name after the village of Rufford – the origins of which are discussed later in this chapter.

Rampton

This name is listed as *Rametone* in 1086 and as *Ramton* in 1198, and is of Old English origins. Here the elements *ramm* and *tun* combine to describe 'the farmstead where rams are kept'. Clearly such places were early wool producers.

Around here we find **Carr Drain** from Old Scandinavian *kiarr* 'the channel in the marsh'. **Butler's Island** would have been dry land in the fen and was associated with George Butler in about 1840. **Fleet Bridge** has its basis in Saxon *fleot* referring specifically to 'a small stream'. **Wranglands Lane** has changed little from the Old English *wrang* meaning 'crooked'.

Ranby

An Old Scandinavian name recorded as *Ranebi* in 1086, as *Ranesbi* in 1098, and as *Raneby* in 1247. Here the personal name is suffixed by the Old Scandinavian *by* and giving 'Hrani's farmstead'.

Ranskill

Another name which shows Nottinghamshire's historical connection with the former Danelaw, the region controlled by the Scandinavians when England was

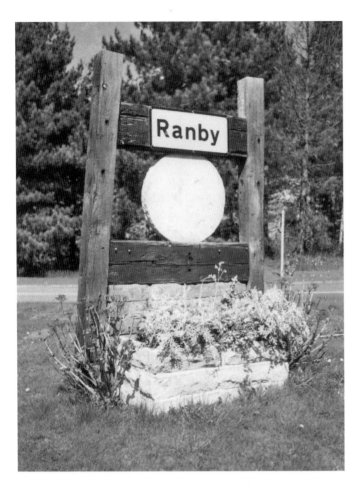

Left: *Ranby village sign.*

Below: *The village sign at Ranskill could have been designed for this book.*

divided between them and the Saxons. Here the name is probably derived from Old Scandinavian *hrafn* + *skjalf* meaning '(place at) the shelf or ridge of land frequented by ravens'. Alternatively the first element here may be a personal name Hralf, used as a nickname. It is recorded as *Ravenschel* in 1086 and *Ravenskelf* in 1275.

There is a **Headland's Lane** here, which is not as simple as it seems for it does not refer to a topographical feature. Here the lane refers to a field with a 'headland', or the strip of land left untouched by the plough to give the ploughman just enough to turn.

Ratcliffe on Soar

As with the name of Radcliffe-on-Trent, this name comes from Old English *read* + *clif* and means '(the place at) the red cliff or bank'. Listed as *Radeclive* and *Radecliva super Soram*, there are similarly named places in neighbouring Leicestershire, hence the addition. This is the name of a river, the origins of which are discussed under its own entry.

As noted many times in the preceding pages, the locals will pull no punches when referring to the less desirable parts of the parish. Some of the 'remoteness' names for the furthest part of the region are usually taken from the farthest corners of the former British Empire and beyond. Similarly when a region was seen as producing little for the efforts of the farmers it was soon labelled accordingly. One name here is a perfect example of the latter. **Drypot Barn** was named after the region on which it stood, a somewhat uncomplimentary name for infertile soil.

Rempstone

Here is a name of Old English derivation in 'the farmstead of a man called Hrempi', the personal name being suffixed by *tun*. It is possible that this is a nickname, for it is known there is a *hrympel* meaning 'wrinkled'.

Many parishes have a 'remoteness' name, a humorous attempt to describe the farthest-flung corner of the parish by naming it after a distant corner of the world. One of the most unusual examples of such a name is found in Rempstone. Indeed it is often thought that the name of **Canaan Farm** has biblical implications, but this is not so except as a likely source.

Retford

There are actually two places named such, **East Retford** and **West Retford**, which have grown and merged to produce just one settlement. Early listings are plentiful and include *Redforde* in 1086, *Retford* in 1230, *West Retford* in 1278, and *Estreford* in 1375. The basic name is of Old English beginnings *read + ford* and speaks of '(place at) the red ford', the colour referring to that of the soil.

Local names here include the somewhat oddly named **Hospital Farm**, so called because it stands on the land where the Trinity Hospital was founded in 1665. Another somewhat unusual name is that of **Plaster Hill**, although there can be no doubt this refers to the gypsum found in this region.

One local recalls the most famous railway locomotive of all time. The **Flying Scotsman** was the first of Sir Nigel Gresley's Pacific class, the flagship of the LNER. Today the engine still runs on preservation lines and special routes throughout the country and has even been abroad. The **Rum Runner** is a name found throughout the land, a reference to the men and the ships which smuggled rum into the country. It hardly seems likely the place was named to show it was where the men hid out or where the contraband was shipped through, thus it probably referred to a man who worked for the customs and who was renowned for catching the smugglers in an earlier career.

Rolleston

A name also found in both neighbouring Leicestershire and Staffordshire, yet the other two feature a different personal name. With records of *Roldestun* in 1086, *Roldeston* in 1219, and *Rollestun* in the late thirteenth century, this is a hybrid of an Old Scandinavian personal name with Old English *tun*. This name means 'the farmstead associated with a man called Hroaldr'.

Near here is an almost circular tributary of the Greet known as **Rundell Dyke**. The Old English *dic* follows Middle English *rondel* or Old French *rondelle* which describes the oddly circular appearance of this watercourse.

Ruddington

With records found from 1086 as *Rodintun* and *Roddintone*, in 1182 as *Rudinton*, and in 1231 as *Rutington*, there is no doubt this is a Saxon personal name followed by Old English *inga + tun*. Thus this name has its beginnings in 'the farmstead associated with the family or followers of Rudda'.

Two local names of note here are **Mickleborough**, which refers to the '(the place at) the big hill', however do not expect to find any large hill here, it is only 'big' in comparison. The name of **Savage's Row** only refers to the surname, descendants of that family are still to be found in the village today. The name comes from France and was used to describe 'someone of fierce countenance', although this should not be taken too literally but seen as referring to a noble and strong countenance.

Trade names feature in pub names and the coat of arms is often used as the sign. One of the most common is the **Bricklayers Arms**, although whether it refers to an early landlord or the customers is difficult to see. **The Jolly Farmers** features a first element which is often used to suggest a pleasant and hearty welcome awaits within. All these 'jolly' names are designed to entice potential customers through the door, although there is no reason to assume that farmers were any more welcome than anyone else.

The name of **The Nottingham Knight** does not refer to any specific individual, it is simply a reference to the castle of Nottingham and the history associated with the city. The name of the **Red Heart** seems to have been derived from the sign, which features a wrought-iron heart which has been painted red. The suggestion is that it represents the heart of Mary I, which may show a Catholic link somewhere in the history of the establishment. The heart is relevant where this monarch is concerned for she was on the throne when Calais was lost to the French, the last of England's holdings in France, and many have quoted the queen as saying that when she died the name of Calais would be found engraved upon her heart.

Rufford

A place which listed in Domesday as *Rugforde*, as *Ruchforde* in 1150, *Ruford* in 1157, and in the modern form as early as 1167. There can be no doubt this refers to 'the rough ford', likely to be a description of the approach and/or exit rather than the bed of the river itself.

Local names here include **Elmsley Lodge**. Listed as *Ummeslowe* in 1335 this began life as '(place at) Immi's burial mound'. The second element of **North Laiths** comes from Old Scandinavian *hlatha* or 'barn'. There is no South Laiths, the village was lost centuries ago, the only surprise being that the remaining name has retained the first element.

As Rufford had its own abbey, there is only one possible explanation for the name of **Pittance Park**. This was land held by the abbey for the endowment of the pittancer, one who was responsible for organising the meagre hand-outs known as pittances. **Toot Hill Wood** has become somewhat corrupted over the years since it was 'the look out hill'.

Former residents are remembered by such names as **Hudsons Hill Wood**, recalling James Hudson and his family who were here by 1850. However, **Roy's Bridge Lane** never did lead to anywhere associated with a man called Roy. The real origin here is Old English *hris* or 'brushwood', which had evolved to become Royce Bridge by 1825.

It is not unusual to find names coined by rivals and neighbours which make derogatory comments about the land or abilities of those working it. While names such as **Hunger Hills** are quite normal, **Labour In Vain** may well be a unique field name.

S

Saundby

Here is a name listed as *Sandebi* from the eleventh century. As this is the only early form we have it makes the first element difficult to define with certainty, although it is certainly of Old Scandinavian beginnings. There are two possible meanings here, the most likely being ''Sandi's farmstead'. However, if this comes from *sandr* + *by* it would give us 'the sandy farmstead'.

Saxondale

Here is a name which helps show what has been quoted several times in these pages, that place names are not coined by those that live there but by a neighbouring settlement. Listed in Domesday as *Saxeden* and as *Saxendala* in 1130, the present name tells us this was 'the valley of the Saxons'. This is from Old English *Seaxe* + *dael*, although it should be noted that Domesday shows the suffix as *denu*, a Saxon word with exactly the same meaning.

As stated, this name would have come from the neighbours, for the Saxons cited would have called this place simply 'home'. Furthermore we know that those in the neighbouring settlement were not Saxons, indeed we can be almost certain they were Scandinavians. Nottinghamshire was on the border between the areas of Saxon England and the region known as Danelaw. Neighbouring settlements from different cultures would have been quite common, particularly after the cessation of any hostilities in a unified England.

Scaftworth

The notable records of this name are few, all we have are *Scafteorde* in 1086, *Seftewurd* in 1185 and *Skaftwurth* in 1341. These forms lead us to three possible definitions of this name. The only element we are certain of is the suffix which, even today, is exactly the same, the original Old English *worth* 'an enclosure'. It should be noted that the Saxon *worth* referred to a defensive feature only in the sense that it offered overnight protection to their livestock.

Here the first element is most likely a personal name. However, as discussed in the previous entry of Saxondale, there were Saxon and Scandinavian influences in Nottinghamshire and the individual concerned could be from either culture. If he was a Saxon this would be 'Sceafta's enclosure', if Scandinavian 'Skapti's enclosure'.

Yet there is a third possibility. There is a chance this may be Old English *sceaft* which would tell us this was 'the enclosure made with poles'. While a man-made fence of poles would be commonplace, most would take advantage of bushes, scrub, trees, and other natural features. If this is the origin it would suggest this defensive feature was constructed entirely of poles and thus would stand out from other every other *worth*.

Locally we find **Delve Drain**, a name meaning 'digging, quarry' and used here to tell us of a purpose-built drainage channel. **Theaker Lane** features a word peculiar to the area, a dialect term for the trade of 'thatcher'. Another trade has been suggested as the origin of **Cobblety Row**, however as the earliest record is as *Cobley Row* in 1840 the likelihood is it refers to the cobbles forming the street rather than it being where the local cobbler lived and/or worked.

Scarrington

Listed in Domesday as *Scarintone*, in 1166 as *Shernintona*, and in 1167 as *Scherninton*, this name has evolved along similar lines to that of the previous name of Scarle. Here again the origin is Old English, but the pronunciation has been greatly influenced by the Scandinavian presence in this region.

While the element -ing- in a modern name is usually indicative of a personal name, the early forms show this is not the case. However, there are two possible origins for this name, the two being quite similar in form and meaning. If this is *scearnig* + *tun* it would tell of 'the muddy or dirty farmstead', while if this is from *scearning* + *tun* the meaning would be slightly different in 'the farmstead at or near the dirty place'.

Lunnon is an unusual name which has confused etymologists for some time. However, in recent years one explanation has gained increasing support. The region lies in an extreme corner of the parish. If, as with many such regions, the locals have coined a remoteness name to describe this area, then it seems likely that the name is a slurred pronunciation of the nation's capital city – London.

Screveton

Listings such as *Screvetone* in 1086, *Screvintone* in 1200, and *Screton in the Clay* in 1323 make the beginnings of this name clear, especially as Domesday's eleventh-century record is so very similar to the modern form – itself something of a surprise. This comes from Old English *scir-gerefan-tun* or 'the farm of or belong to the sheriff'.

Scrooby

A name of Old Scandinavian origins listed as *Scrobi* in 1086, *Scroby* in 1225, and *Scruby* in 1242. Here the common element *by* follows the personal name as 'Skropi's farmstead'. **Neale's Covert** was named after residents Thomas and William Neale or one of their relatives, who were here by 1840.

Selston

With records of *Salestune* in 1086, *Selestun* in 1249, and *Selveston* in 1277 it is not clear which Saxon personal name is followed by Old English *tun*. This is either 'Sele's farmstead', or 'Seli's farmstead', but without further examples it is unlikely we will ever be certain which.

Around the parish are a number of names worthy of note. **Bagthorpe** is derived from 'Baggi's outlying village', the personal name here is likely to have been a nickname, and not a particularly complimentary one. The delightfully named **Beaufit Farm** is not what it may seem, for the origin is Old Danish *bothj*, quite literally 'booth', and *thveit* 'parcel of land', so this is understood as 'the dwelling of the small estate'. **Hobsic** is an unusual sounding name for a place, yet it probably comes as no surprise to find it refers to 'the goblin stream' and speaks of the haunting by a sprite or similar supernatural being.

Mexborough does not take its name directly from the place in Yorkshire. While it does come from the town meaning 'Meoc's fortified place', it was brought to Selston by a resident of both places, William de Mekesburgh, who was here in 1332. Other personal names over the ages have produced places such as **Wansley Hall** being 'Waendel's woodland clearing' since before the Norman Conquest, **Hill Banks** was home to William del Hill in 1332, **Allen's Green** was home to Anthony Allen in 1636, and from the map of 1840 we see that William Dodson and Henry Lilley were living at **Dodson's Row** and **Lilley's Row** respectively.

Selston's **Bulls and Butcher** is a little different in having more than one animal. However, the meaning is still that this was where animals were slaughtered. The pub and the butcher's were probably separate arms of the family businesses.

Shelford

A name seen in Domesday as *Scelforde*, in 1155 as *Sceldford*, in 1232 as *Scelford*, and in 1276 as *Scheldford*. Despite some sources linking this name with the site of a shelter used by hunting parties, there is no doubt this comes from Old English *sceldu* + *ford* and is '(the place at) the shallow ford'. While it might seem pointless describing a ford as 'shallow', for any depth would make fording the river improbable, a great number of names quite often state what is obvious.

Shelton

Early records are not unlike that of the modern form as *Sceltun* and *Scelton*. However, we are still able to see this as coming from Old English *scylf* + *tun* or 'the farmstead on the shelf of land or ridge'.

The name of **Wensor Bridge** would have stumped us were it not for a record dating from 1330. The modern name is much abbreviated from the fourteenth-century *Wendelford brigge*, itself derived from 'Wendel's ford'.

Sherwood Forest

A name which is probably as synonymous with the county as that of the county town. This name comes from the Old English *scir* + *wudu* and speaking of the 'wood belonging to the shire'.

The oldest record we have been able to trace is as *Scirwuda* in 955, with *Scyryuda* just three years later. It should be remembered that a number of the trees which make up this forest are known to be older than this.

Great thought goes into the signs welcoming drivers to this village.

Shireoaks

It hardly seems necessary to define this name; it means exactly what it says. Indeed, it means more than what it says for it tells us this is the '(place at) the oak trees on the county boundary'. A comparatively recent name, it is first found in the twelfth century as *Shirakes*.

Sibthorpe

This may or may not be a hybrid name, it depends upon which of the very similar personal names involved forms the first element. Listed in Domesday as *Sibetorp* and in the twelfth century as *Sibbetorp*, neither form shows clearly which language provided the beginnings but do confirm the suffix is Old Scandinavian *thorp*.

Either this is the Saxon 'Sibba's outlying farmstead', or the Danish 'Sibbi's outlying farmstead'. Without further evidence this is likely to remain unknown.

Here we find the quite extraordinary sounding name of **Deadwong Lane**, a comparatively recent name from the late Middle English describing 'the poor soil of the piece of meadowland'.

Skegby

A place near Mansfield listed in 1086 and 1227 as *Schegebi* and *Skegeby* respectively. This is an Old Scandinavian name of one origin with two possible meanings. Here we find the personal name with *by* and giving 'Skeggi's outlying farmstead'. However, the lack of the possessive 's' could show this is *skegg* 'outlying farmstead on the beard-shaped promontory'. It is obvious where the personal name originated, although it does raise the question as to what Skeggi was called before he was old enough to grow a beard!

Local names of note here include **Healds Wood**. From the Old English *hielde* meaning 'slope', the name has clearly been mistakenly (and quite understandably), thought to have been a personal name which acquired the possessive 's'. The name of **Marshall's Parlour** is derived from its association with resident George Marshall in 1661. Another name of interest is **The Brand** meaning 'the place where burning takes place', not an horrendous form of execution but simply where charcoal-burners were known to work. Before coal was mined, charcoal was a fuel source and was created by smouldering wood under a mound of earth. It took time to perfect the skills required to stack the wood correctly under the mound so that the fire did not go out but nor did it flare up and burn away. This was a slow and very tedious task which did not allow the charcoal-burner the luxury of sleep, despite it taking days rather than hours. In order to prevent them sleeping on the job, they would seat themselves on stools with a single leg. If they should fall asleep they would fall off their stool and awaken, which is where we get the expression to 'drop off' meaning to fall asleep.

One pub here is known as the **Forest Tavern** which is a reference to Sherwood Forest, rather than the usual 'foresters' who worked there. Perhaps it was one of the trees from this ancient woodland which provided the wood for the **Maypole** which, in turn, gave its name to the pub. As the name suggests this was the focal point for May Day celebrations in the village. Bedecked with streamers, a complex and ornate pattern would be created by the movements of the dancers.

The **Rifle Volunteer** is a name which recalls a former landlord or inn-keeper. A volunteer soldier would not have been funded by the government of the land, indeed in order to be accepted by the armies of the day they had to provide their own weapons and pay for tuition to an acceptable standard before being allowed to fight.

Smite

A very common river name indeed, although the vast majority are minor watercourses, little more than ditches. There are a number of words from various tongues which may have been the original for the stream name. However, the most likely explanation is that they all had some influence, which depends upon the era and the location of the river.

Nottinghamshire's Smite could have come from Old English *smitan* 'to glide', Middle English *smite* 'to move rapidly', Old Swedish *smita* ''to slip away', or several others. Whichever the language, the meaning is obvious; this river was simply described as 'moving' and visibly so.

The upper reaches of the Smite were formerly known as the Coker. This, like Cocker Beck, comes from the British or Celtic word *kukro* meaning 'crooked'. At Aslockton there is a **Cocker Bridge**, the only surviving reminder of the former river name.

One tributary of this river is the **Winter Beck**, clearly a suffix from Old Scandinavian *bekkr* meaning 'spring'. Thus the name seems to indicate it is dry during the summer months. However, this is not the case. While it is true that in times of drought there is little to be seen, it never dries out completely. Hence this is most likely an exaggeration, although there is a possibility that changes in the contours of the land, or even the climate, have altered the character of the river.

Sneinton

A name recorded as *Snotintone* in 1165, *Snoiton* in 1208, *Snenton* in 1242, and *Sneington* in 1254. This place has a name derived from the same personal name as the county town and the county itself, this being 'Snot's settlement'. Any idea that this is the same person should be considered highly improbable. The name of the city of Nottingham is listed as early as the ninth century, while Sneinton is not seen until three centuries later. This does not mean the name did not exist earlier, but it was simply not recorded, possibly because it was too small. Even if the two places were named around the same time, it is still highly unlikely to have been the same person for people simply did not travel to any extent.

Locally are names such as **Peas Hill**, which described that part of 'the hill where pease grows'. Obviously less was thought of another slope where 'the hill poor with pasture' became known as **Hunger Hill**.

One man who would probably have had more pubs named after him had he not commanded the British fleet during the American Revolution was **Earl Howe** (1726–99), more favourably remembered for his victory in the battle against the French on the Glorious First of June, the first engagement in the Napoleonic Wars to be fought at sea.

The Lamp is not as common a sign as it once was, principally because the reference is to a gas light which no longer is powered. Today it is difficult to find a Lamp with an actual lamp, normally they display a painted sign. **The March Hare** originally comes from the lagomorph which really has earned its title of being 'Mad' during the courtship season (not strictly confined to the month of March). Most inns have exploited the association with the character from *Alice in Wonderland* by Lewis Carroll for the sign hanging outside. The **Oakdale** takes its name from the road leading here, although it seems the road likely took its name from a field name of obvious origins.

Soar

A tributary of the Trent which joins it near Thrumpton at the Trent Locks. Listed as *Sora* in 1322 and *Sore* in 1330, it is a British river name probably meaning 'the flowing one' and related to the *Saar* in Germany.

Sookholme

The earliest listings of this name are found as *Sulcholm* in 1189, *Sulegholm* in 1193, *Sulcheholm* in 1287, and *Sokam* in 1557. This shows how Nottinghamshire place names have been influenced by both the Scandinavian and Saxon languages. Here Old English *sulh* combines with Old Scandinavian *holmr* to give '(the place at) marshy land in the valley'.

South Scarle

Here is a place name which reveals more than a meaning while looking for the origins. For a change we will take the distinguishing addition of 'South' first, for this is the simplest part. There is a North Scarle, just over a mile away and, as stated, to the north. However, it does not really belong in this book as it is in neighbouring Lincolnshire.

The name of Scarle comes from the Old English *scearn + leah*, which would have evolved as something closer to Sharnley or Sharley were it not for the influence of Scandinavian pronunciation. This evolution tells us that the name was coined by Saxons but, as the name was likely to have been given by a nearby settlement, was used more often by Scandinavians.

Two places so close together sharing a name shows that one is an offshoot of the other. Here the southern settlement seems to be the original settlement, and thus the place which the name describes. This means '(the place at) the dirty woodland clearing'. Usually we would see this as either telling of somewhere particularly muddy or even a place with copious amounts of dung.

It is odd to think that any settlement would deliberately foul their homes to the point where it would give rise to its name. A better explanation might be that the second settlement was created because of some flood or other unavoidable disaster which befell the original. However, the most likely is that the name was simply an insult, created by neighbours from a different culture who were also traditional foes.

Southwell

Even today this name tells of its origins, to us even more clearly than records of *Sudwella* in 958, *Sudwillum* in 1000, and *Sudwelle* in 1086. Indeed this name is for the '(place at) the south spring' and comes from Old English *suth + wella*.

North-east of the town, running along the appropriately named **Riverside**, is the **River Greet**. Here it provides a boundary between the town and Normanton, before heading off to join the Trent. The two earliest records we have of this name both come from the same year of 958, as *Greotan* and *Grete*. Clearly this is from the Old English *greot* meaning 'gravel'. It would be easy to think of this as a river with a gravel bed, however it simply has never flowed swiftly enough to scour the bed of its accumulation of mud and water plants. Thus the name must have originally been given to land passed by the river. Hence this fairly lengthy river, for its size, was named from a region of just a few hundred yards at most.

To the west of the town is a region known as **Westhorpe**. Despite the loss of a 't', this is certainly 'the outlying farmstead to the west', from Old English *west + thorp*. It has also given its name to a small tributary of the Greet, **Westhorpe Dumble**. The term *dumble* is Middle English used in general terms to describe 'the wooded valley' or 'trees along a stream' when referring to a more specific area. As streams and rivers are nearly always named for their appearance or character in a particular area, the latter definition would be the most likely.

Around the region we find a wealth of minor place names which tell us something of that locale throughout the history of the settlement of Southwell and its surrounding lands. **Buckhill** can still be seen as being named for 'the hill frequented by bucks' and is one of several 'hill' references in names hereabouts. **Hockerwood** is an Old English name describing 'the hump hill wood', while **Cundy Hill** is more recent, coming from Middle English *conduit* and telling us of 'the water channel', most likely purpose-built for irrigation and/or a source of fresh water.

The name of **Holbeck Farm** is derived from *holh bekkr* 'the place of the stream in a hollow'. Individuals are remembered in **Calvert's Farm**, home of Edwin Calvert by

1840, **Ferne's Folly** reminds us that Henry Ferne was here, also in 1840, and was a neighbour of Thomas Trebeck, who left his name to **Trebeck Hall**.

The name of **Burbage** has historically been a distinctly separate self-contained area. It was that part of the town not held by the church, being deliberately left to provide a place for the vital market place for the trading community, thus bringing prosperity to the region. Perhaps one of the traders who sold his wares here was living at **Saversick Lane**, a name telling us this was 'the soap maker's lane' a skill which produced soap from a base of wood ash.

Street names include **Palmer's Yard**. Sir Matthew Palmer was the most prominent member of the family who had an estate in nearby Easthorpe. **Rope Walk** and **Ropemakers Lane** recall the early nineteenth century when ropemakers were operating in the town, Wilkinson's being the largest family business in this area. **Squires Pond** is all that remains of the land owned by Doug Squires, who started off life as a farmer and later lived as an agricultural merchant. The area around here was donated by the Squires' estate for wetland conservation.

Of all the names associated with Southwell's history, few can merit the honour of having places named after them than he who gave his name to **Edward Cludd School**. Today it is part of the Minster School, yet when it was built it was independent. The man in question was MP for the area during the mid-seventeenth century. A succesful London businessman in his own right, he was a mercer of Lombard Street. However, his best known act was when he saved the minster from serious damage during a conflict with Parliamentarian and Scots troops.

The Old Coachhouse is one of the few of its kind to have later taken on a name speaking of its earlier life as a staging post. **The Saracen's Head** is a symbol taken from a landed family whose ancestors were allowed to display such having fought in the Crusades. The **Hearty Goodfellow** displays a sign featuring the jolliest of chaps, hoping to attract others inside to partake of their wares.

Undoubtedly there was once a **Bramley Apple** tree standing next to the pub of that same name.

Spalford

The first element here is actually more common than we would expect, particularly found in minor names. This comes from Old English *spald* + *ford* 'the ford across the trickling stream', and is recorded as *Spaldesforde* in 1086, *Spaldeford* in 1183, and as *Spaldyngfordwath* in 1329.

Stanford on Soar

A fairly common name which always originates from Old English meaning 'the stony ford'. Indeed it is because the name is such a common one that there has been an addition. This is the river which is crossed, the Soar, which means 'the flowing one'. It is listed as *Staineforth upon Sowre* in 1521.

Stanton on the Wolds

Listed in 1086 as *Stantune* and in 1240 as *Stanton super Wold* this name is undoubtedly from the Old English for 'stone enclosure', a literal term referring to naturally occuring stony ground. The addition is from the Old English *wald*, a term used only around Nottinghamshire and its bordering counties, referring specifically to 'high forested land which had been cleared for use'. It seems this addition was to make it stand apart from Staunton in the Vale.

Page's Lodge was built on land associated with former resident John Page and his family, who were here by 1850.

Stapleford

A name found throughout England, usually as a minor name. It is derived from Old English *stapol* + *ford* and describes the '(place at) the ford marked by a post'. This place is found as *Stapelton* in 1203 and *Stepleton* in 1242.

Under Nottingham's entry is listed the name of the pub named after Sir John Borlase Warren and noted his achievements. At Stapleford the same gentleman is depicted as a young man in navy uniform with his future bride outside the Happy Man. Thus not only has a local hero been honoured but a suggestion of happiness being found within has been made. Named after the classic British car, the Jaguar shows a rather splendid earlier model on its sign.

Staunton in the Vale

Listings have been discovered as *Stantone* in 1086, *Staunton* in 1269, *Stanton in le Vale* in 1535, and *Staton 'ith Vale of Beaver* in 1657. The basic name is a common one, speaking of 'the farm on or by stony ground', hence the addition which clearly refers to the Vale of Belvoir, itself a name derived from the Old French for 'beautiful view'.

Locally is found Mar Plantation, a name which refers to the 'boundary plantation' found on the outskirts of the parish.

Staythorpe

Listed in 1086 as *Startorp*, in 1196 as *Staretorp*, and *Stathropp* in 1594. This is from an Old Scandinavian name telling us this began life as 'Stari's outlying settlement'.

Stoke Bardolph

A name recorded in Domesday as simply *Stoches*, in 1197 as *Stokes*, and in 1208 as *Stok*. Other records show something closer to the modern form, such as *Stokes Doun Bardul* in 1194, *Stoke bardulf* in 1269, and *Stoake Bardall* in 1656. This features the Old English *stoc*, the most common place name in England and meaning 'special place'. It is often said the *stoc* was a place of worship or was said to have some magical significance to the owners. However, if the word is defined as 'specialised' we are less likely to expect anything wondrous, being content to accept it being a place of metalworkers, or even where one crop was farmed exclusively. Obviously whatever was considered special was pertinent only to those who named it such, a reason we are unlikely to discover.

The addition refers to the manorial holding by the family of William Bardolf, who was here personally by 1235.

Stokeham

As a standalone place name element, Stoke is the most common in the land, thus it is normally found with a distinguishing second element or, as here, forming part of a longer name.

Stokeham is first seen as *Estoches* in Domesday, with later records of *Stokum* in 1242 and *Stocum* in 1303. While there may seem to be two elements here, it is actually an evolved form of the fourteenth-century record, where *stocum* is plural and refers to '(the place at) the outlying farmsteads'.

This should not be taken as being a farmstead, indeed it was probably nothing of the sort. The term is used to refer to a place of special importance, for a variety of reasons. Thus it may have been where the workers of these outlying farmsteads met on the regular day of worship at this, an impromptu place of worship. It seems likely that these were, at least initially, temporary or seasonal settlements.

A record from 1850 tells us Frank Beardsall was in residence at what is today known as **Beardsall Farm**, while not the animal but William Otter's name was the basis for **Otter's Farm**.

Strelley

Early records include *Straleia* in 1086, *Stratlega* in 1168, *Stradeleie* in 1169, *Stretlei* in 1175, *Stralleg* in 1196, *Stredlega* in 1201, *Stritlegh* in 1265, and *Styrley* in 1539. Despite the odd modern form, the early records certainly suggest this is from Old English *straet leah* or 'the woodland clearing by the Roman road'. However, there has never been any evidence of a Roman road around here, yet this is no reason to doubt the origin.

Another name here, which also has questionable origins, is that of **Cat Stone**. It is said that the lump of a conglomerate rock is said to resemble the shape of a cat. Obviously this depends on the viewpoint of the observer and, even if standing in the right place, still requires a good imagination.

Stroom Dyke

A small tributary of the Smite which derives its name from Old Scandinavian *straumr* and speaks of 'the stream'.

Sturton-le-Steeple

Records of this name are found as *Estretone* in 1086 *Strettun* in 1236, while the addition is not seen until as late as the eighteenth century with *Sturtton le Steeple*. This is a name from Old English *straet* + *tun* meaning 'the farmstead on the Roman road'. While the addition clearly refers to the church tower, it does seem rather late and somewhat unnecessary. While there are two other Sturtons, both are in Lincolnshire and not particularly close by at all. It is true that there is a noticeably straight road connecting two, yet the most likely reason for this late addition was to make the road signs more decorative.

Locally we find **Fenton**, a name which means exactly what it seems 'the settlement in the fen' from Old English *fenn tun*. There is also **Holmefield**, the first element comes from Old Scandinavian *holmr* 'the marsh meadow' while the latter 'field' is a modern addition of obvious meaning.

Styrrup

This place is listed in Domesday as *Estirape* and clearly erroneous, so we turn to the later record of *Stirap* in 1197. Undoubtedly, here is Old English *stig-rap*, literally 'stirrup' and a reference, not to the place, but to the hill east of the village thought to resemble that familiar shape by early residents. Thus it was the name of the hill which was later transferred to the settlement.

Local names include **Farworth**, a combination of Old Scandinavian *vath* 'ford' by an Old English *faer* literally meaning 'going, passage'. Combined, this reference is to the ford and the track on either side of it. The first element of **Oldcoates** has been corrupted; this name began life as 'cottages where owls are seen'. The cottages, logically, cannot always have been old.

Even today the name of **Clatticar** still has a very Scandinavian sound to it. However, only the second element here is from that tongue, *kiarr* meaning 'marsh'. This is preceded by a Lincolnshire dialect word clatty meaning 'dirty'. While it is difficult to see how a marsh can be described any other way, it is not unusual to find an addition to a basic name stating the obvious. Such additions are commonly found when the other element comes from a different language and the meaning is unknown.

Sutton Bonington

There are almost more Suttons in England than can be counted. This is hardly surprising when we learn of the simple origins of the name, for all come from Old English *suth* + *tun* 'the southern farmstead'. Obviously all such places were named by occupants of a settlement roughly to the north.

The vast majority of additions are manorial, used to differentiate when the basic name is found nearby or is a common one. Here, however, is a name which evolved naturally for this was originally two distinctly separate places as evidenced by Domesday's record of both *Sudtone* and *Bonniton*. This second settlement has a name derived from an Old English personal name with *inga* and *tun*, giving 'the farmstead of the family or followers of Bunna'.

It should not be thought that there was any official union of the two. Being in such close proximity they would have shared a lot of natural resources, including intermarriage. The most obvious place to build the new home would be between the two, thus over a period of time they simply merged to form one place. It is easy to see this, even today the place is greatly elongated even more than would normally be expected. In fact it is most likely that the settlement to the north, from which Sutton got its name, was Bonington. The most surprising thing is to find both names retained, we would normally expect the simpler Sutton to have been lost.

Locally is the name of **Zouch Mills**, an Old English nickname for poor quality land which is sometimes defined as *sot* meaning 'soot' or by others as *sott* 'foolish'. Without sufficient records, which are not going to be traced for such a minor name, it is difficult to know which is the meaning, yet the message is ostensibly the same.

St Anne's Lane was named after the church dedicated to this saint. **Bucks Lane** was named after the eighteenth-century farmer and local constable with the delightful name of Hart Buck. Many villages have a central area of grass, indeed the village green is as much a part of traditional English life as any thing else. It is often the location for many village celebrations as indeed it was on the night of VE Day in May 1945 when a bonfire was lit on the green and the celebrations went on late into the night. That night was permanently etched on the village for the grass beneath the bonfire never grew again, thus **The Green** is not as 'green' as it was when named.

Sutton-in-Ashfield

As with the previous name the basic name is the simplistic 'southern farmstead'. This place is recorded as *Sutone* in Domesday, the affix not seen until 1276 as *Sutton in Essefeld*. This is, as discussed under the entry of Ashfield, 'open land where ash trees grow' and has been added for distinction.

The name of **Fulwood** is of Saxon origin meaning 'the foul or dirty wood', a somewhat exaggerated description of a very muddy place. Similarly **Harlow Wood** is thought to be derived from *horh hlaw* meaning 'the dirty hill', although it could have quite a different meaning if the Old English beginnings are *hord hlaw* or 'treasure hill' – amazing what a difference one letter can make.

Henning Lane comes from the later Middle English language, where *haining* described a 'protected pasture enclosure'. **The Siddalls** is found throughout the counties of the Midlands and is derived from Old English *sid healh* or 'the wide nook or corner of land'. **Carsic Lane** existed centuries before the combustion engine was ever thought of, hence it has nothing to do with travel sickness but comes from Old Scandinavian *kiarr sik* or 'the little stream by a marsh'. Indeed the little stream was effectively little more than a natural drain. Finally **Greenhill Farm** does not refer to a pasture on a slope, but would have been where the family of Matilda de Grenehull originated, although she was here by 1331.

Today the modern shopping centre is known as **Idlewells**, which comes from the stream as a water source and was taken from the name of **Idlewell Place**. The stream name is discussed under its own listing.

Club Row took its name from the club room of the Old Trooper Inn, the entrance to that room in the former public house being from that street.

Cursham Street remembers the family who lived at Ashleigh House, while **Haslam's Hill** is named after the very busy family who provided a range of services to the community as builders, joiners and even undertakers.

Scott's Hole is named after resident Nanny Scott, who dug the hole here to enable her to dye materials, then still a cottage industry. Polly Tomlinson, who lived in Spring Alley, was such a well known figure that the area around her home became known as **Polly's Niche** which was eventually adopted as the official name by the borough. **Bennett Street** was named after the family who have lived in the town continuously since 1579 when Roger Bennett came here to marry Katherine Emery. **Langforde Street** recalls the family who lived at Manor Farm, surgeon Anthony

Langforde (died May 1672) is buried in the local church. The **King William the Fourth Inn** was unusual in that it did not display Roman numerals as the regal number. Perhaps this was down to one owner, a Mr S. Bower who is remembered by the name of **Bower's Yard**.

Parliament Street was constructed near an ancient meeting place, at one time known to the locals (somewhat unkindly) as Wayster Lane! **Wood Street**, which led past the wood rather than to it, was formerly known as Blind Alley on account of the familiar figure of Blind Tom being in residence. **King Street** was named as such in 1660 at the Restoration of the Monarchy, prior to which it was known by the rather ignominious name of Beggar Street.

Gadsby's Yard remembers the family who owned the property here. Thomas Gadsby died in 1791 aged forty-two while his wife Rosamund lived on until 1827 to the ripe old age of eighty. Their son Matthew enlisted with the 13th Light Dragoons, fought in the Napoleonic Wars and was present at the Battle of Waterloo. He then travelled out to the East Indies to continue his military career. In recent years the name has been changed to **Sherwood Yard** and while the etymology is obvious, the reasons for any change are obscure.

Downing Lane was named after a family who lived here, all having a reputation for being extremely long-lived. Records show some members of the family did live to good ages, however they also had as many who died in infancy as any other residents. Samuel Downing's daughter Frances married the Revd Clement Nott, a Baptist minister who was here by 1837 and who gave his name to **Nott's Yard**.

The **Denman's Head Hotel** was formerly known as the King's Head. However, in 1820 the trial of Queen Caroline, a story which held everyone's attention for its entire duration, was the scandal of the day. Landlord Mr W. Cooper was as pleased as the rest of the nation when she was acquitted and immediately changed the name of the place to honour the name of her defence, a Mr Denman, who went on to become Lord Justice Denman.

The **King and Miller** refers to a traditional local narrative. The monarch in question was Henry II, who had lost his way in the great forest of Sherwood. He stumbled upon a miller who offered him refreshment, including a meal of venison. Normally this would have resulted in the miller being arrested, for only the king was allowed to hunt these deer. However, King Henry was amused by the event and later made the miller Sir John Cockle. **Workpeople's Inn** is clearly a name intended to attract those of lesser stature than Henry II.

Sutton on Trent

If proof was required of the number of Suttons in England, here is a third example in Nottinghamshire alone. Again 'the southern farmstead' here takes its name from the river, the name of which is discussed under its own entry.

Local names here include **Sternthorpe Farm**, which has its origins in 'Stjarni's outlying village' and features an evolved personal name form the nickname 'Star' which also features in the name of Staythorpe. **North Holme** and **South Holme** feature obvious compass point references preceding Old Scandinavian *holmr* or 'marsh meadow'. A William de Holm is recorded as being here in 1332, who in all likelihood, took the family name from this place.

Barrel Hill is an isolated feature with a distinctive and obvious shape. **Dunstall Lodge** features a corruption of the Old English *tunsteall* which can be defined as 'farmsteading', while **Smithy Marsh** has nothing to do with metalworking but is actually derived from Old English *smethe eg* meaning 'smooth island' and a reference to the marshy land here.

Syerston

Both Domesday's record of *Sirestune* and the later *Siristun* from 1236 show this to be a Saxon personal name with Old English *tun*. Thus we are able to define this name as 'Sigehere's farmstead'.

T

Teversal

An intriguing name, particularly considering that the meaning is uncertain. Indeed there are three possible definitions here, all of which are of Saxon or Old English beginnings and are listed as *Tevreshalt* in 1086, *Tivresholt* in 1204, *Thiversold* in 1275, *Tyversolde* in 1280, *Tyversald* in 1290, and *Tyversalt* in 1291.

It is tempting to suggest a personal name followed by *hald* giving 'Teofer's shelter'. However, this first element could also be seen as *tiefrere*, a word which is used to describe either a 'painter' or even sometimes a 'sorcerer'; an interesting combination indeed.

Dunsill has changed little from its beginnings as '(the place at) Dunn's hill'. **Fackley** is less certain and could either be from Old English *fealh leah* 'the fallow clearing', although more likely *fah leah* giving 'the stained or variegated clearing', a reference to a mottled colour of the soil rather than the vegetation. The same suffix is found in **Stanley** which is 'the stony woodland clearing'.

A fairly common minor place name comes from Old English *new bold* meaning 'the new building', seen here as both **Newbound Farm** and **Newbound Mill**. Meaning '(place at) the hill where wheat grows' is **Whiteborough** from Old English *hwaete beorg*.

Thoresby

Recorded as *Yuresby* in 958 and as *Turesbi* in Domesday, here is a name of Old Scandinavian origins. The suffix here is the most common in the region once known as Danelaw, *by* being the quivalent of Saxon *tun*. Thoresby began life as 'Thurir's farmstead'.

It is interesting to note that this place has no distinguishing addition, yet in neighbouring Lincolnshire there are two further places, North and South Thoresby.

This is probably because the Lincolnshire Thoresbys have origins in a different personal name and have evolved along quite different lines.

Thorney

A name found in other places in the land from Old English for 'thorn tree island'. However, Nottinghamshire's version has a subtly different suffix, as evidenced by early records of *Torneshaie* in 1086, *Thornehawe* in the twelfth century, and *Thornhaghe* in 1282, this is from *thorn* + *haga* or 'the enclosure formed by thorn bushes'.

Local names here include **Drinsey Nook**, the first element here is the Old Scandinavian *drengr* meaning 'young man, or servant'. This can be understood to be 'the nook of land worked by the young men'. **Markbush Wood** is on the county boundary; the name identifies this important fact.

Thoroton

Here we find a name of Scandinavian and Saxon origin; the former a personal name, the latter the common suffix *tun*. This is 'Thorfrothr's farmstead', formerly recorded as *Toruertune* in 1086, *Turueton* in 1177, and *Thuruerton* in 1242.

Thorpe in the Glebe

Recorded as *Torp* in 1086, *Bochardistorp* in 1235, *Thorphynchlebys* in 1268, and *Thorpe in the Clottes* in 1287, there is clearly a decided difference in the names of the thirteenth century. Today the name is derived from the Old English *thorp* meaning 'outlying farmstead'. The addition may be either Latin *gleba* or French *glebe* meaning 'clod of earth', and a reference to land difficult to work for whatever reason. The other records from the twelfth century are alternatives for the same meaning, with the exception of the name of *Bochardistorp* which refers to it being held by John Bochard.

Another former resident of this village is remembered by **Annabell's Farm** which, despite what it may seem, is in fact a corruption of the name of John Annible's family who were here by 1850.

Thrumpton

As with the previous entry, here is another name featuring a Scandinavian personal name with the Old English suffix *tun*. Here the record of *Turmodestun* is found in Domesday, evidence that this was formerly 'Thormothr's farmstead'.

Biggins Farm may give an impression of being from a personal name, however the real basis is the Old English *bigging*, telling us there must have an unusual or distinctive 'building' here. Likewise **Whisker Hill** has nothing to do with animals but is a corruption of 'white scar hill'. We also find the names of **Wrights Hill**, which takes its name from the occupancy by the family of Edmund Wrighte, who were here by 1596.

During the Middle Ages a system of agriculture was in use when traditional ploughs moved the soil only to the right. Over the years this produced a series of ridges and furrows as the soil built up in some areas and was removed from others. Although there was no standard stipulated width for a plough, the practical use of it meant it could not be too wide and yet the farmers obviously wished to optimise the time spent ploughing. The resulting ridges and furrows were a signature as to the width of the field, thus the number of ridges would often identify the field and this is how **Twenty Lands Plantation** got its name.

All Saints' church, Thrumpton.

Thurgarton

Yet again, as with the previous names, a Scandinavian personal name is followed by Old English *tun*. What was *Turgarstune* in Domesday began life as 'Thorgeirr's farmstead'.

Locally we find **Magadales Farm**, which was named from an unknown tenant as being 'Margaret's valley farm', while the name of **Coneygre Farm** tells us this was 'the rabbit warren' and features the term *coney* the original name for the rabbit.

The local here is the **Red Lion**, the most popular pub name in England. This is of heraldic origins; very early names would be a reference to John of Gaunt while later the reference is to Scotland.

Tithby

The Old Scandinavian *by* is as common in regions of that culture's influence as the Old English *tun* is where Saxons were dominant. Indeed both have similar meanings, where both can be seen as 'farming community, village'. Clearly at a time when communities were almost self-sufficient, agriculture was the most important part of daily life and such a name could be applied to virtually every place in the land, hence these suffixes are so common throughout the land.

As the suffix *by* is so common, a defining second element is required. In this case it is a personal name and produces the meaning of 'Tidhe's village'.

Tollerton

Domesday records this place as *Troclauestune*, later *Torlauetun* and *Turlaueston* in the twelfth century. As with the previous entries, this is another Scandinavian and Saxon hybrid, here beginning life as 'Thorleifr's farmstead'. It should be noted that another Tollerton, in North Yorkshire, has a quite different first element in *tolnere* giving 'farmstead of the tax gatherers'.

Within the parish we find **Bassingfield Farm**, the name was brought here by John de Basyngfeld from the district a few miles away near Holme Pierrepoint. Here this is a family name which is taken from a place name meaning 'the open country of the people or followers of Basa'.

Torworth

Another Scandinavian and Saxon hybrid, the suffix here being Old English *worth*. Records of this name abound, from *Turdeworde* to *Thorchewurh* in 1275. There are at least five forms so far discovered, all of which show this to be 'Thorfthr's enclosure'.

Toton

A name which is derived from an Old Scandinavian personal name Tofi and the Old English *tun* or 'Tofi's settlement'. The listings of this place are many and varied and include *Tolvestone* in 1086, *Touuiton* in 1235, *Tofneton* in 1271, *Tauton* in 1428, *Toweton* in 1489, and *Toveton* in 1612.

One local pub here was named in 1959, shortly after the space age began with the launching of Sputnik. The **Other Side of the Moon** is something which had never been seen at the time and even today suggests somewhere most people would be intrigued to see.

Treswell

An Old English name recorded as *Tireswelle* in 1086 and *Tyriswell* in 1242. The first element here is a personal name followed by *wella* and giving us 'Tir's spring or stream'.

The river here is the **Lea Beck**, which exhibits two elements from different languages. Here Old English *lei* combines with Old Scandinavian *bekkr* to give 'the flowing stream'. The Saxon name must have already been in existence when the Scandinavians added the suffix during the period when Nottinghamshire was a part of the region influenced by the Danelaw.

Other local names include **Stanhope Farm**, the earliest relevant record dating from 1327 when the name of John de Stanhop is mentioned. Clearly this person was already associated with a place known as Stanhope (yet there is no record of this name in the region any time before this), while the obvious meaning 'stony valley' simply does not belong here. The only possible explanation is that John was already known by this name and brought it with him when he arrived in Treswell. The most likely origin for this transferred name, Stanhope, is a village east of Durham; even though this is over a hundred miles north, it does follow the most direct route along the Great North Road. However, it will never be possible to say for certain.

Outgang Lane features the Middle English element *wong*. Here it is used in combination with the element 'out' and refers to 'the piece of land taken from the meadow', the lane itself would have run alongside rather than to the place. **Turn-a-Beck** is a name which has become corrupted within the last two centuries, for it was recorded as *Turner Beck Close* in 1840. The name refers to a field held by the Turner family some time before this date, while the beck or stream is either lost or a mere drainage ditch. It is highly unlikely to be an alternative name for the Lea Beck, for it would have to be extremely localised and even if the family knew their part of the river by that name, it would never have stuck.

Trowell

Early forms of this name differ little from that of the modern spelling. Found as *Trowalle* in Domesday and *Trowella* in 1166, this name comes from Old English *treow* + *wella*. Defining this name gives a mental image of the place in Saxon times for the literal meaning of 'tree stream' suggests a settlement near where a tree trunk was used as a bridge.

A couple of field names here remember former residents of Trowell. Robert Shaw was here in 1624 and Elizabeth Potter in 1739, leading to the names of **Potter's Plantation** and **Shaw's Plantation** respectively.

The local **Festival Inn** remembers that, following the Festival of Britain in 1951, the village received a special award for being typical of a British rural community.

Tuxford

A name found in Domesday as *Tuxfarne*, with *Tukesford* in 1212, and the modern spelling as early as 1316. Despite these forms the first element is uncertain. This may

Village sign at Tuxford, first erected in the thirteenth century for the market, re-sited in 1897 and restored in 1997.

be the case of another Scandinavian personal name followed by Saxon *ford* and thus is 'Tuk's ford'. However, there is growing support for this to be from Old English *tusk* + *ford* and telling of '(the place at) the ford where tussocks or tufts of rushes grow'.

While there can be no doubt that **College Farm** refers to the land being held by Trinity College, Cambridge, the origin of **Rebel Stone Close** is difficult to understand. Several stories have been told about the 'rebel', none of which are found prior to the road being constructed and are based purely on that road sign.

Any field or close with a stone name could be understood two ways. The most common is a reference to small stones which makes ploughing difficult, although in such circumstances the place name would be expected to show an adjective as 'stony'. Secondly this could be a single larger stone and this seems more plausible. Furthermore, this may offer a definition for the 'rebel' element. If this were such a sizable stone to make moving it impossible, with the technology available at the time, then it could be seen to be rebellious, particularly so if it was one of several and the only large stone which refused to budge! Although this is pure speculation and has no evidence to back it up, this name was far too intriguing to simply ignore completely.

Tuxford's working mill.

U

Underwood

The earliest record here dates from 1287 as *Underwode*. It may seem a name of obvious origins, yet the first element is not literally what it might seem. The true origins here are Old English *under* + *wudu* referring to the '(place) within a wood'.

Upper Broughton

A name which has acquired its addition fairly recently, to differentiate from nearby Nether Broughton. It is listed as *Brotone* in 1086, *Brohton* in 1205, and *Brotton* in 1276. There can be no doubt this comes from the Saxon meaning 'brook farmstead'.

Locally is **Muxlow Hill**, named after resident Mr Mucklow who was here by 1689 and whose family doubtless brought this place name with them.

Upton

A very common name, indeed it is unusual to find it standing alone for it usually has a second defining element. However listing such as *Uptune* in 958, *Upetune* in 1086, *Uppeton* in 1167 and in the modern form of *Upton* as early as 1185 show this has never been known otherwise. This name is always from the Old English *uppe tun* or 'the higher farm'. While it may seem obvious that this refers to a place standing in an elevated position above another, the place where the settlers likely first came from, it more likely refers to its standing in terms of wealth and/or power, rather than geographically.

Walesby

There is a similarly named place in neighbouring Lincolnshire. Because they are some 40 miles apart and in differing counties, no distinguishing addition has been required. This is a name of Old Scandinavian origins recorded as *Walesbi* in Domesday. The suffix is *by* and follows a personal name, giving 'Valr's farmstead'.

Two local names may, at first glance, be easily misunderstood. For example there must have been many speculative tales told about **Hanging Hill Plantation**. However, while the noose cannot be said to have been or not been used at some time here, it certainly has had no influence on the name. The 'hanging' here is used to mean 'overlooking hill', not necessarily 'overhanging' in the sense we would understand today but simply a vantage point over the main settlement below.

The second minor place name has likely not only been misunderstood but probably corrupted by the same misunderstanding. Going back to a record dated 1794 we find **Nickerbush Plantation** listed as *Nickhagh bush*, which has two possible beginnings. The safe option would be to suggest *nick hagi* or 'the enclosure with a notched gap' and the bush mentioned being a marker. However, there is a second alternative which would carry more weight were it not based on a former dialect word used solely around this area. The term 'Nicker' was used in the Nottinghamshire/Lincolnshire region to refer to a woodpecker and, although it has fallen out of favour, may well have been used to describe this place, thus the record from the late eighteenth century could be erroneous. Doubtless there have been other suggestions for the origins of this name in more recent times. However, these will not be touched upon here.

Walkeringham

The element -ing- is a good indicator that the preceding element is a personal name. Indeed the listing in Domesday as *Wacheringeham*, with *Walcringeham* in 1212 and *Walcringham* in 1316 show this to be an Old English personal name followed by *inga* and *ham*. This place began life as 'the homestead of the family of followers of Walhhere'.

Within this region, the minor names include **Line Croft House**. This place is named after the area in which it was built, first found in 1300 as *Lingcroft* and from the Old English *Hlinc*. This gives us the definition of 'small farm on or by the hill'. **Wooden Beck Hill** actually means 'the stream by the lost place of Wotton', while the place name refers to 'the settlement by the wood'. **Millbaulk Road** features the Middle English element *balke* giving 'the path on the ridge to or near the mill'. Local families are also featured, including **Cave's Lane** which is associated with the family of William Cave who was known to be living in neighbouring Misterton in about 1689.

Warsop

Domeday lists this place as *Wareshope*, with later records of *Warsopa* in 1180 and *Warshop* in 1233. Here is a Saxon personal name followed by Old English *hop* and telling us of 'Waer's place in the valley'.

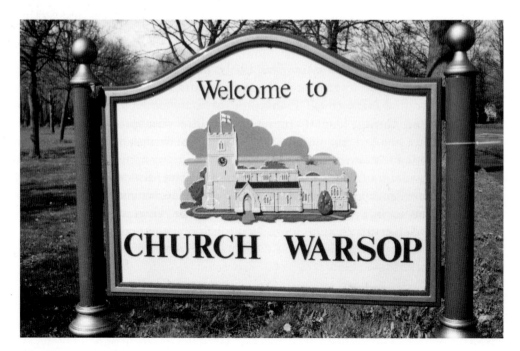

The district of Church Warsop.

The Carrs at Warsop, an old Scandinavian name speaking of the waters here.

Gleadthorpe Grange comes from Old Scandinavian *gletha thorp* or 'the outlying farmstead where kites are seen'. This reference is to the bird, not the toy. **Nettleworth Manor** features the Old English *worth* and began life as 'the enclosure overgrown with nettles', presumably not the most desirable place to be. Other names recall former residents, evidence for which is found in a document of 1689. This record gives the names of William Norman and Widdow Turner whose family gave their names to **Norman's Plantation** and **Turner's Plantation** respectively.

Watnall

This name is found as Watenot, Wattenho, and Watenho in 1086, 1200, and 1205 respectively. This shows a name with its origins in a Saxon personal name and Old English hoh, meaning this place began life as '(place of) Wata at the hill-spur'.

Welbeck

Records of this name are found as *Wellebech* in 1161, *Welebec* in 1201, *Wilebek* in 1270, and *Welbecke* in 1284. Here are two elements, Old English *wielle* and Old Norse *bekkr* both of which refer to the same stream. This watercourse rises at Creswell in Derbyshire and flowed to the Poulter above Norton, while today it feeds an artificial lake.

Locally is the name of **Roomwood**, describing the woodland as 'spacious', more a suggestion of being well-spaced rather than covering a large area.

Welham

Although there is a place with an identical name in neighbouring Leicestershire, the two have different origins. Here the Old English word for the place is *wellum* which is plural and means 'the springs'. Of course the name was probably in existence before the settlement was founded here, which in turn took on the same name. Hence we should give this as '(place at) the springs', and note there is no Saxon *ham* or 'homestead' here as proven by records of *Wellun* in 1086 and *Wellum* in 1242.

Wellow

Location can have a strong influence on the development of a name. Wellow could never be termed as being common, yet a number are dotted around the land. There are a number of different meanings and several quite different origins. This can be seen by comparing this place with its namesake on the Isle of Wight which comes from *welig* 'willow tree'. The Nottinghamshire version, listed as *Welhag* in 1207, comes from Old English *wella* + *haga* or 'enclosure by a spring or stream'.

Resident families have left their mark on local place names. **Cocking Moor** recalls John Cocking who was here in 1701 and **Jordan Castle** was the residence of Jordan Foliot in 1252 when he was granted permission to increase the defences of the manor house by the king. It is somewhat unusual for the man's christian name to be taken for a place name when there is a surname. **George Dyke** may also seem to follow the same pattern but in fact the basis is 'gorge' not 'George', even if the feature is not as grand as the current understanding of the term would suggest.

Grimston Hill is an interesting name and worthy of some attention. Although we have some records of this name they are few and not particularly early. This suggests the name was coined comparatively late which, for a geographical feature, is unusual. Of course it could be that this was not the original name, in which case the suggestion of 'the settlement of a man called Grim' is quite likely for this is a common personal name for Norsemen.

Yet it may be that the first element is from the same tongue as the suffix. Indeed if the settlement or *tun* is preceded by the Saxon *grim* then this would tell us the place was deemed to be haunted for that is the Old English for 'a ghost'.

One pub here is named the **Red Rover**. It is not unique for there have been a handful of former coachhouses which have taken the name of one of the country's most famous stage coaches. However, the name was also given to a number of ships and to the children's game which evolved from British Bulldog.

West Bridgford

Domesday's record of *Brigeford* shows the meaning as well as today's version, it is simply 'the ford by the bridge'. Of course this does raise the question as to what the place was called when there was just a ford across the river, although there is no surviving record of a place here earlier than 1086. The additional 'West' needs no explanation, other than to say it was to differentiate from East Bridgford. The record from 1238 leaves us in no doubt as to where this Bridgford is to be found for it appears as *Brigeford juxta pontem de Notingham*.

West Burton

Obviously, given the number of Burtons, a defining second element is often required. Here it simply tells us this was to the west of another settlement, not necessarily another 'fortified farmstead' but probably the leading settlement in the vicinity. Also here is the local name of **The Ferries**. Often thought to be a mispronounced 'fairies', it in fact comes from a family name. The earliest known resident is Christiana de Fery in 1332, yet it seems certain she was not the first of her family to put down roots here.

Weston

This is a simple enough name to define. This is 'the west settlement' – in this case west in relation to Normanton.

Here is **Scarthing Moor**, an Old Scandinavian name from *skratti* 'goblin' and *hagi* 'enclosure', and suggesting that the moorland was considered to be haunted.

West Stockwith

The first element here is additional, to distinguish from the other Stockwith which is in neighbouring Lincolnshire. Listed in the twelfth century as *Stochithe* and

Road sign at Scarthing Moor on the Great North Road near Weston.

Stokehede, here is a name from Old English *stocc* + *hyth* and is '(place at) the landing site made of treestumps or logs'. There is also the minor name of **Stockwith Ings**, the addition coming from Old Scandinavian *eng* or 'low-lying grassland'.

Here we find **Heckdyke**, a name recorded as *Hecdike* in 1298, and *Hek dike flu* in 1575. This is a name which gives us a snapshot of life in Saxon times, simply by defining its origin. The term dyke is still used today with the same meaning of water channel. However, *heck* has evolved to become 'hatch', a trap for fish made from a combination of wicker basket traps and piles or stakes.

Whatton

Records of this name are rather sparse, but the identical name is found in neighbouring Leicestershire and has very similar beginnings. Therefore it is probably safe to state that this comes from Old English *hwaete* + *tun* and was 'the farmstead where wheat was grown'. Domesday lists the place as *Watone*, but the name tells us almost as much as the eleventh-century census. Norman officers record this was held by Robert from Gilbert de Ghent. It had a mill and millstone quarry. Defining the name tells us wheat was grown here, and grown for season after season in order for the name to stick. During Saxon times barley was a much more common crop than wheat; it was easier to grow. This therefore also tells us something about the soil quality and the skills of the farmers. More importantly to the author of this book, it conjures up an instant image of life in Saxon times, an image which will outlast any photograph or painting.

The **Moor Dyke** is the local stream, a name which comes from Old English *mor* meaning 'marsh' and the addition the ditch which drained it. The **River Whipling** is recorded as *Viplin* in 1140. This has been suggested to be from Middle English *whippen*, which can be seen in the sense 'to whip' when defined as 'to move briskly'. However, this tributary of the Smite could never be described as 'brisk', at times it is difficult to even see it is moving at all. Furthermore, the twelfth-century record is a little early for a Middle English origin, albeit much of that language is very close to its predecessor of Old English. Without further evidence the origin of this name remains uncertain.

Wheatley

Everything that applied to Whatton applies here. The difference in the name is the suffix, here Old English *hwaete* and *leah* combine to tell us of '(the place at) the clearing where wheat is grown'. Listed in Domesday as simply *Wateleie* there are actually two places in Nottinghamshire with this name. Known as **North Wheatley** and **South Wheatley**, the two are separated only by the width of the road.

At North Wheatley is **Freeman's Gorse**, once associated with George Freeman and his family who were here in about 1840. There is also the strangely named **Klondyke**, which is another of those 'remoteness' names and a humorous reference to its location at the extreme south-west corner.

South Wheatley features the former **Oswald Beck**, a stream which ran from here to the Trent near Bole. The name is Old Scandinavian and speaks of the '*bekkr* (stream) of Asverthr'. **Muspitt Lane** is first found in 1840 and refers to 'the hollow where moss grows' which would have been alongside the lane rather than where the path led. While **Blue Stocking Lane** does not have any basis in the disparaging term for an intellectual or successful woman, it was a likely influence for there is no other basis for the colour appearing in this name. From the Middle English *stocking*, this name refers literally to 'the stump clearing', a place where the stumps of trees were either to be removed or had been.

Widmerpool

This place is found in Domesday as *Wimarspol*, in 1181 as *Widmerepol*, and as *Widmerespol* in 1186. Here is a name which has two potential meanings, both of Old

English derivation. Either this first element is *wid* with *mere* 'the wide lake', or it could be *withig* and *mere* 'willow tree lake'. The suffix is evidence that the confusion is not only contemporary, for it is from Old English *pol* meaning 'pool'.

Locally is found **Morris's Plantation**, named after former resident Robert Morrys whose family were here by 1533.

Wigsley

With a Saxon personal name followed by Old English *leah*, this is '(the place at) the woodland clearing of a man called Wicg'. Records have been traced listing this place as *Wigesleie*, *Wiggesle*, and *Wigesle* in 1086, 1160, and 1257 respectively.

Wilford

A name listed in Domesday as *Wilesford* and as *Wileford* in 1190. Here the two Old English elements of *wilig* and *ford* combine to tell us of '(the place at) the ford by the willow trees'.

Willoughby on the Wolds

The name of this place is recorded as *Willebi* in 1086, *Wilgebi* in 1130, *Wilehebia* in 1226, *Wilghebi* in 1258, and *Wylughby* in 1342. This comes from an Old English and Scandinavian combination describing the 'willow village'.

Normally additions are to differentiate from similarly named places nearby. While this is not a unique name, the nearest other Willoughby is in Warwickshire. As discussed elsewhere it is a regional name from *wald* describing 'high forested ground which has been cleared'. As the addition is comparatively late it was likely added for other unknown reasons.

Locally we find the name of **Bryan's Lane**, a reference to former residents James and Alice Bryan who were associated with this place by 1778. A name which began life as 'Secgge's wold' has evolved to become **Six Hills**, although this seems to have been deliberately corrupted otherwise this would almost certainly have become Sex Hills!

Winkburn

There are two equally plausible definitions for this Old English place name, which has records of *Wicheburne* in Domesday and *Winkeburna* in 1150. It is often given as a personal name with *burna* and peaking of '(the place at) Wineca's stream'.

However, if the stream name existed before the settlement it could not possibly be a resident who had yet to arrive, but would come from *wincel* + *burna* or 'the stream with bends'. The latter seems increasingly logical but, unless earlier records are found, the name will remain uncertain.

To complicate matters further the name of the river in question is currently the **River Wink**. Considering what has been said about the place name this cannot be considered to be the original name of the river. Any earlier name is unrecorded, while the modern version is simply back-formation from the place. It seems this is a much harder question to answer than that of the chicken and the egg.

A minor name here is **Roe Wood**, which comes from the Old English *ra haga* or 'the roe deer enclosure'.

Winthorpe

While Scandinavian and Saxon hybrid names are by no means uncommon, it is rare to find the Saxon element being the personal name. Here the suffix is Old Scandinavian *thorp* and it is more likely that the personal name is also from that culture and is 'Vigmundr's outlying farmstead' than the Saxon alternative of 'Wigmund's outlying farmstead'.

Wiseton

A place recorded in Domesday as *Wistone* is also found as *Wiston* in 1212. These forms are quite alike and, with no other listings remotely early enough to be of assistance, it makes the first element uncertain. It is no surprise that one alternative is a personal name, given to be 'Wisa's farmstead' with a Saxon personal name. However, the name could come from the Old English elements *wisc* and *tun* or 'the farmstead by the marshy meadow'.

Of the many local names here, two reveal something of the past. One recalls the family of Michael Bland, here in 1689 and after whom **Bland's Wood** is named. The second is more mysterious, particularly as today there is no known legend associated with this place. However, in the past there must have been some tradition tied to **Drakeholes**, for the name of the place comes from Old English *draca* meaning 'dragon'.

Wiverton Hall

Listings of this name are found as *Wivretune* in 1086, *Wiuertone* in 1180, and *Werton* in 1387. There can be little doubt this comes from 'Wigfrith's farmstead'.

Wollaton

Records of this name are plentiful. In 1086 it is *Olavestone*, in 1156 *Willonestune*, in 1235 *Wllavetun*, in 1236 *Wullaueton*, in 1276 *Wolatone*, in 1280 *Wolhafton*, and in 1488 *Wollaghton*. However, these many forms, and others, still make it difficult to give the personal name with any degree of certainty, although it will probably not be much different to 'Wulflaf's farmstead'.

One local pub is named the **Hemlock Stone**. This is a reference to a landmark nearby, a red sandstone rock of unusual shape. **The Wheelhouse** is a name usually associated with the sea although it can also be a reference to a barn or similar storage area where a wheelwright kept his goods.

Woodborough

An Old English name recorded in Domesday as *Udeburg*. A name which comes from Old English *wudu* + *burh* speaks of 'the fortified place near the wood'.

Within this region we find an Old Scandinavian place name, evidence Woodborough was influenced by both cultures. Here **Bonner Hill** is derived from *brunnr haugr* which translates to 'the hill with a spring'. However, the Saxon tongue prevails when naming **Grimesmoor** or 'the moor of a man called Grim'. This personal name is also a word which refers to a sprite or ghost, hence it could be that the moor was thought to have been home to a supernatural being. However, maybe it is used here as a nickname, likely a derogatory term, suggesting the individual was possessed (probably insane).

The original name of **Nags Head** was given to inns where a traveller could hire a horse to continue their journey. The mount would have been a stocky and sturdy animal, although never would it have been described as a thoroughbred. It would be ridden to the next place and could be changed to continue on a fresh animal. In the days when horse-stealing was a capital offence, only the most desperate would ever consider stealing the horse.

Worksop

The self-styled 'Gateway to the Dukeries' gets its name from 'Weorc's place in the valley'. The personal name is suffixed by the Old English *hop* and is listed in Domesday as *Werchesope*. The Dukeries refers to the 150,000 acres south of the town which was set aside during the eighteenth century for forest land, country estates and associated villages. The region was originally administered by the dukes of Newcastle, Portland, Kingston, Norfolk and Leeds (hence the name) and remains an area of special beauty.

Worksop Priory.

The district of **Bassetlaw** is noted in Domesday as *Bernesedelaue* which seems to originate from Old English *baernet* + *saete* + *hlaw*. If this is the correct origin, which is by no means certain without further examples, this place was 'the place at the hill of the land dwellers by the burning'. This suggests the land was cleared by fire. What is more it also tells us that the remains of this fire must have been visible for some time, for it is rare for any short-lived feature to find a basis in a place name. Perhaps a larger region was destroyed than was ever utilised for farming, or possibly it is telling us that the fire got out of control.

As mentioned elsewhere in this book, the longer rivers and streams must at one time have had more than one name. The simplistic nature of river names mean they always reflect what the residents see in any one locale. Clearly the longer rivers flow past a variety of landscapes and flora, and thus will likely have had several names once. As soon as any one name was committed to a map then this name became fixed. In Worksop is the district of **Rayton**, a name where the suffix is Old English *tun* 'farmstead'. The first element here is a variation of Rea, a common Middle English river name from *attere* 'at the river'. However, the river name here is not the Rea but the **Ryton**, which comes from the place name, a process referred to as back-formation, albeit somewhat corrupted. To complicate matters even further, an earlier name for this river was the *Blyth*, another example of back-formation from the village of this name which also stands on the banks of the river. Which came first is difficult to say. Indeed it seems highly unlikely that any of these names are the original, which would have been given during the Celtic era or even earlier.

Interesting local names around Worksop abound. Some speak of the history, others of its former residents, while there are also those describing the regions around here during the period often referred to, somewhat unfairly, as the Dark Ages.

Street names of Worksop include **Bridge Street**. Listed as *Bryggegate* it is fairly obvious this road has led north to the river crossing for centuries, although today it is closed to traffic and is mostly pedestrianised. Although **Broad Lane** may not seem to live up to its name today, when it was first coined in about 1840, maps show it was substantially wider than other roads. **Cheapside** is a name found in most towns throughout the land and is often misunderstood. The name is from the Old English *ceap* meaning 'market place' as can be seen from the fifteenth-century record of *le Merketsted*.

A long-established milepost at Worksop.

Gates at Clumber Park.

Church Walk is another name of fairly obvious meaning, and indeed it means what is says. However, the listing of *Kyrkegate* is relevant for other names found in the town. The suffix in the old record of -gate does not have the same meaning in a place name, it is from the Old Norse *gata* meaning 'roadway'. If we look to define it more as 'the way to', it can be seen to fit both the Saxon meaning and the modern definition. Knowing this, the roads named **Eastgate** and **Newgate Street** speak for themselves, although in the latter example the additional 'street' shows the meaning of *gata* was unknown even during the eighteenth century. One further name, **Potter Street**, has been known as such since 1692. Prior to this, as late as 1636, it was *Potter Gate* and has the same origins as the similar names. The first part could refer to the trade although it more likely refers to an individual whose family name was taken from there.

Bracebridge is a region listed as *Wersbrighill* in the thirteenth century, *Bersebrigga* in 1316, and *Brasbrige* in 1541. It is an ancient forest area, yet the name may be as recent as Middle English, coming from *berse*. If this is the origin it would speak of an enclosure where a series of hedges were reinforced by stakes – which tells us the hedges were insufficient and probably newly planted specifically for this purpose.

Clumber House here is derived from two elements, the river name with Celtic *bre* giving '(place at) the hill by the Clowne'.

Listings as *Derffeld* in 1305, *Dirfeld* in 1383, and *Derfold* in 1528 show the origin to be Saxon *deor feld* or 'open land of the animals' where wild animals would gather and has been corrupted to become **Darfoulds** today. Other animals gave their name to **Gateford**. Despite what it may seem, and what was said regarding street names such as Eastgate and Newgate Street, the first element here is Old English *gata* with *ford* and not the Old Norse word. The early forms of this name include *Gattef* in 1130 and *Gaiteford* in 1166, which show the influence of the Old Norse *geit* showing this to be 'the ford used by goats or where they are seen'. The question of how we can tell the difference between languages when the word is identical is an obvious one. In response there are two clues, firstly the ending is Saxon *ford* and not Norse *vath*, and the combination giving the meaning 'the way to the ford' is simply not found.

Hardwick is from the Old English *heordwick*, literally 'the herd of the dairy farm'. It is recorded as *Herthewik* in 1280, *Hertheyk* in 1286, *Herthewich* in 1316, and *Herdewic* in 1316. **Manton** is *Mennetune* in Domesday, *Mantone* in 1300, while the modern form appears as early as 1316 and means 'Manna's farmstead'. **Scofton** is recorded as *Skofton* in 1280, *Sckofton* in 1286, and *Schofton* in 1316 meaning 'the farmstead of Skopti'. Here an Old Norse personal name precedes Old English *tun*.

There is a **Rayton Farm** which does not take its name from the district of Rayton, yet has doubtless been influenced by it. Recorded as *Rouuetone* in 1086, *Reueton* in 1287, and *Ryveton* in 1327, it is derived from Old English *(ge)roefa tun* or 'the farmstead of the reeves', an adminstrator or bailiff of a high-ranking official. There is also a **Thievesdale Farm** around here which, quite obviously, has its origins from individuals who were less than respected. As has been said elsewhere in the book, places are named by neighbours, not by those who live there, and thus the 'farmstead in the valley of the thieves' is probably not a literal but a derogatory term. **Sloswick Farm** is an unusual name from the Old English *sla* 'sloe' and *wic* 'specialised farm'. Although the normal specialised farm is seen as a dairy farm, the definition of *wic* here is unlikely to be this and can only be guessed at. Thus the meaning should be given as 'the farmstead by the sloe thicket'.

The name of **Holme Carr** is derived from the Old Scandinavian *holmr kiarr* and is listed as *Le Holmker* in 1305 and as simply *Holmker* eleven years later. This tells us of 'the island in the marsh meadow' and is the raised land within two branches of the Ryton river. **Tranker Wood** took its name from the adjoining piece of land recorded as *Traneker* in 1340. This is an Old Scandinavian name from *trani kiarr* meaning 'the marshland frequented by cranes'.

Osberton Hall stands on land recorded as *Osbernestune* in 1086 and as *Osbertona* in 1227. This points to an origin of 'Osbern's farmstead' which we know to be the Old Norse name Asbjorn, as used by Anglo-Saxons. **Bridge House** is listed as the home of one *William ad pontem de Wyrkesop* in 1302, and a name of obvious origin. **Kilton Hill**, home of Huge del Hul in 1287, is derived from the Saxon 'Cilla's settlement by the hill', with the Scandinavian influence changing the initial letter.

A region associated with less welcome members of society, though maybe not entirely accurate.

Other individuals who have left their name on the landscape include Edward Ashton, who was here by 1586. Christopher Chapman was living next to **Champions Plantation** in 1636, two centuries before **Eddison Plantation** was home to John Eddison and **Sharpe's Hill** to Jarvis Sharpe.

Trees are, compared to human lifetimes, extremely long-lived and therefore become viewed almost as permanent sights in the landscape. Thus, as with even longer-lasting topographical features such as rivers and hills, trees have given their names to places. Indeed sometimes they actually become markers, such as with the place now known as **Shireoaks**. Listed as *Schirokes* in 1160, *Skyrakes* 1280 and *Shirakes* in 1286, this refers to oak trees which still stand here on the border between Nottinghamshire and Yorkshire.

Scratta Wood still sounds Scandinavian today. Indeed the name comes from two Old Norse elements *skratti* 'goblin' and *hagi* 'enclosure', which should be seen as 'the haunted enclosure'. A third 'tree' name is a little different. At first it would be reasonable to think that the first element of **Streetley** is the Saxon *straet* referring to a Roman road. However, the records of *Stiueteley* in the thirteenth century and *Styteleye* in 1322 show this to be from *styfician* 'to root up' and *leah* 'clearing'. The sense here should be seen as a place in the wood where not only the trees were cleared but, unusually, the stumps of those felled trees too.

The names **Forest Screed** and **Grotto Screed** feature the element *screed* which is from late Middle or early Modern English and refers to a strip of land. This word seems to be a dialect term found only in Nottinghamshire and the neighbouring counties of Yorkshire (when it was one county) and Lincolnshire. The additions of 'forest' and 'grotto' mean exactly as they would seem, as does **Hawks Nest Screen**, although the dialect term had already been corrupted by 1825 when the name is first recorded.

Other field names around Worksop include **Busaco**, named after the battle of 27 September 1810 when the British under Lord Wellington defeated the French led by Marshal Massena in the Peninsular Wars. Predictably **Coach Road Plantation** stands alongside what was a coach road leading to the town, the plantation being named such in about 1825. Finally there are two fields named from their shape, **Halfmoon Plantation** and the delightful name of **Ale Bottle Clump**.

Streets around Worksop also reflect the history of the place, none more so than **Beaver Place** which reminds us that the town has long been associated with the production of beaver hats. Another local industry is commemorated indirectly. **Clinton Street** recalls the Clinton Kilns which stood here. These were used to roast the barley prior to brewing.

Duke Street refers to the Duke of Newcastle, lord of this manor, whose seat is the basis for the name of **Clumber Street**. Another name of aristocratic beginnings is that of **Manvers Street** from the Pierrepoint family, Dukes of Manvers.

The road taken by a family to their lands and home.

Smithhurst Row was another of the many roads throughout the land named from the developer, as indeed was **George Street** which recalls Mr George Mayor, son of a local butcher who started working for a solicitor's office before becoming an auctioneer and ultimately a property developer. **Watson Street** remembers Sir Henry Watson, a man who worked in the legal profession and who hailed from Sheffield.

Boundary Row actually takes its name from the Boundary Inn which was here in the 1840s when it was the parish boundary. **Dock Road** is something of an over-statement, for it allowed access to the coal wharf of the local colliery and John Grafton's boat yard, a man who was honoured by **Grafton Street**.

The river of that name was the basis for **Ryton Street**.

Finally we come to John Colbeck, a man who did as much as anyone to merit a street being named after him. He was signed as an apprentice by the millwright Thomas Cuckson. By the time the owner had retired, Colbeck had risen through the ranks to take over the reins himself. Not that he ever forgot his beginnings; he was often known to remove his jacket and work alongside the men. Many was the time he worked until after midnight to complete an order due out the next day. Despite working six days a week he was not idle on the Sunday, walking many miles in his role as local preacher for the Wesleyan Church. Such has resulted in the honour of the naming of **Colbeck Street**.

The pubs of Worksop have taken their names from a number of sources. The **Queens Head** depicts the unmistakeable face of Queen Elizabeth I, a popular name unlike that of the **Three Legged Stool** which is almost certainly unique. Opened in 1978 it stands on the site of a former dairy, hence the milking stool reference. Inside there is a further reference, where the conveniences are designated for the use of Milkmaids and Cowmen.

Wysall

Another of those names which reveal a snapshot of life in Saxon times. This place is recorded as *Wisoc* in 1086, *Wisho* in 1199, *Wisou* in 1236, and as *Wisow* in 1242. This is an Old English name telling us of 'the hill spur with the heathen temple', having its origins in the elements *wig* + *hoh*. It also tells us it was not named by the inhabitants, but was known as this by a Christian culture.

Common Place-Name Elements

Element	Origin	Meaning	Element	Origin	Meaning
ac	Old English	oak tree	*ea*	Old English	river
banke	Old Scandinavian	bank, hill slope	*east*	Old English	east
bearu	Old English	grove, wood	*ecg*	Old English	edge
bekkr	Old Scandinavian	stream	*eg*	Old English	island
berg	Old Scandinavian	hill	*eorl*	Old English	nobleman
birce	Old English	birch tree	*eowestre*	Old English	fold for sheep
brad	Old English	broad	*fald*	Old English	animal enclosure
broc	Old English	brook, stream	*feld*	Old English	open land
brycg	Old English	bridge	*ford*	Old English	river crossing
burh	Old English	fortified place	*ful*	Old English	foul, dirty
burna	Old English	stream	*geard*	Old English	yard
by	Old Scandinavian	farmstead	*geat*	Old English	gap, pass
ceap	Old English	market	*haeg*	Old English	enclosure
ceaster	Old English	Roman stronghold	*haeth*	Old English	heath
cirice	Old English	church	*haga*	Old English	hedged enclosure
clif	Old English	cliff, slope	*halh*	Old English	nook of land
cocc	Old English	woodcock	*ham*	Old English	homestead
cot	Old English	cottage	*hamm*	Old English	river meadow
cumb	Old English	valley	*heah*	Old English	high, chief
cweorn	Old English	queorn	*hlaw*	Old English	tumulus, mound
cyning	Old English	king	*hoh*	Old English	hill spur
dael	Old English	valley	*hop*	Old English	enclosed valley
dalr	Old Scandinavian	valley	*hrycg*	Old English	ridge
denu	Old English	valley	*hwaete*	Old English	wheat
draeg	Old English	portage	*hwit*	Old English	white
dun	Old English	hill	*hyll*	Old English	hill

Element	Origin	Meaning	Element	Origin	Meaning
lacu	Old English	stream, watercourse	*steinn*	Old Scandinavian	stone, boundary stone
lang	Old English	long	*stapol*	Old English	post, pillar
langr	Old Scandinavian	long	*stoc*	Old English	secondary or special
leah	Old English	woodland clearing			settlement
lytel	Old English	little	*stocc*	Old English	stump, log
meos	Old English	moss	*stow*	Old English	assembly or holy
mere	Old English	lake			place
middel	Old English	middle	*straet*	Old English	Roman road
mor	Old English	moorland	*suth*	Old English	south
myln	Old English	mill	*thorp*	Old Scandinavian	outlying farmstead
niwe	Old English	new	*treow*	Old English	tree, post
north	Old English	north	*tun*	Old English	farmstead
ofer	Old English	bank, ridge	*wald*	Old English	woodland, forest
pol	Old English	pool, pond	*wella*	Old English	spring, stream
preost	Old English	priest	*west*	Old English	west
ruh	Old English	rough	*wic*	Old English	specialised, usually
salh	Old English	willow			dairy farm
sceaga	Old English	small wood, copse	*withig*	Old English	willow tree
sceap	Old English	sheep	*worth*	Old English	an enclosure
stan	Old English	stone, boundary stone	*wudu*	Old English	wood